COOPERATIVE VENTURES IN THEOLOGICAL EDUCATION

James W. Fraser
Monica Ellen Friar
Barbara Anne Radtke
Thomas J. Savage, S.J.
Katarina Schuth, O.S.F.

UNIVERSITY
PRESS OF
AMERICA

Lanham • New York • London

Copyright © 1989 by

University Press of America,® Inc.

4720 Boston Way
Lanham, MD 20706

3 Henrietta Street
London WC2E 8LU England

British Cataloging in Publication Information Available

Library of Congress Cataloging-in-Publication Data

Cooperative ventures in theological education /
James W. Fraser . . . [et al.].
p.   cm.
1. Theological seminaries—United States—Cooperation.
I. Fraser, James W., 1944–
BV4163.5.C66   1989   207'.73—dc20   89–34140 CIP

ISBN 0–8191–7490–4 (alk. paper)

All University Press of America books are produced on acid-free paper.
The paper used in this publication meets the minimum requirements of American
National Standard for Information Sciences—Permanence of Paper for Printed Library
Materials, ANSI Z39.48–1984.   ∞

TABLE OF CONTENTS

LIST OF TABLES AND FIGURES

PREFACE

The study team is pleased to present the results of its research on cooperative ventures in theological education. The research is itself a product of cooperation. The names of the authors are listed in alphabetical order. With such a listing, the study team hopes to reflect the contribution of each member and claims equal authorship for each member.

As with any research, time did not permit the study team to visit all possible sites and exhaust all interview and literature leads. However, the study team was especially pleased with the number of responses to its survey and the care and consideration of the respondents. Furthermore, the team is indebted to those who were interviewed. The fine and gracious contributions of so many persons are themselves a collaborative effort and are very much appreciated.

This study was made possible by the generosity of The Lilly Endowment and the superb leadership exercised by Robert W. Lynn and Frederick Hofheinz. Their special care for the future of cooperative ventures in theological education provides a critical source of support.

While the study team acknowledges the cooperation and support of so many persons and institutions, it takes the final responsibility for the statements in its report.

Arlington, Massachusetts
December, 1988

I. Introduction

In 1984 the Lilly Endowment awarded a grant to The Cheswick Center for the purposes of studying the experience and practice of cooperative endeavors in theological education during the past twenty years and recommending some future directions for this enterprise. The emphasis was to be on: 1) assessing past experience in order to identify critical factors that have favored or hindered cooperative ventures, and 2) analyzing the current environment in order to identify what strategic choices are available for the future.

To accomplish this assignment, Cheswick assembled a team of five researchers to examine cooperative activities in theological education. The study team used a strategic planning approach to its work as it set out to accomplish the following:

— develop through documentation and preliminary interviews an initial descriptive profile of the history of cooperative ventures in theological education, particularly the consortium movement, its goals, vision, structure, and current situation;

— assess through questionnaires and site interviews the strengths and weaknesses of existing cooperative efforts and the threats and opportunities represented by internal and external constituencies and environmental trends;

— test basic assumptions and hypotheses about inter-institutional cooperation in theological education held by key leaders, opinion makers, and authors in the field;

— formulate strategic options for the Endowment and test these against findings from the questionnaires, site visits, analysis of the dynamics of cooperation, expectations of potential grant recipients, and competing claims on both the Endowment and its constituencies; and

— recommend strategic choices and the elements of a grant making strategy for the Endowment in the area of cooperative ventures in theological education.

A. Methodology of the Study

The research team used a combination of qualitative and quantitative approaches to collect and analyze information about cooperation in seminaries. The primary instruments used were 1) mailed questionnaires sent to seven individuals at each of the 195 member, associate, or candidate schools of the

1

Association of Theological Schools (ATS) and 2) individual interviews with personnel in schools throughout the United States and Canada. The questionnaire was designed to poll the ATS schools about the extent, motivations, benefits, and problems with cooperation among their schools and other institutions. The interviews were designed to supplement the survey data and to develop in-depth profiles of cooperation at selected institutions.

The methodology used for development and implementation of the questionnaire parallels that of Jackson Carroll and his research team in their 1980 study assessing the programs and services of the Association of Theological Schools.[1] The current questionnaires were constructed after a review of the literature on inter-institutional cooperation among schools of theology and also among secular schools of higher education and were revised after a number of interviews with seminary educators, consortium directors, and researchers were conducted. [See Appendix I for samples of the questionnaire.] From these sources, initial categories and hypotheses concerning cooperation were incorporated into the survey.

A pilot questionnaire was then distributed to ensure that all response possibilities for prescribed questions were offered and to refine the language. Seven copies of the final instrument were sent to the chief executive officer (CEO) at all of the ATS accredited, associate, or candidate schools for completion and distribution by the CEO, the chief academic officer (dean), faculty council leader, student council leader, librarian, registrar, and board chairperson. Each questionnaire had its own return envelope so that confidentiality of responses was maintained.

The CEO, dean, and registrar were given three-part questionnaires. All others completed a two-part questionnaire. Part I of all questionnaires surveyed respondents for the types of cooperation in which their institutions participated. Space was left for the respondents to describe the arrangements in their own words and to add ventures beyond the designated categories. Part II of all questionnaires except that of the board chairpersons asked respondents: 1) to list the one or two cooperative ventures that were most significant for their schools; 2) to identify, evaluate the success of, and predict the future direction of a subset of activities (such as cross registration, faculty hiring, field education) found in most of the significant ventures; and 3) to explain factors which affected their participation in the venture. Part II of the board chairperson's questionnaire addressed the board's role and attitude concerning cooperative ventures. Part III of the CEO and academic dean's questionnaires addressed issues of the future direction of cooperation in theological education. Finally, Part III of the registrar's questionnaire asked for specific information about enrollment, cross registration, and the tuition policy at the institution.

A total of 1365 questionnaires were mailed out, but the total possible returns were fewer since all schools did not have all the positions indicated. For this reason, twenty-five of the questionnaires were returned unanswered and the study team estimates that another twenty-five were not returned because no person occupied the position. In all, 514 questionnaires were returned for a response rate of thirty-nine percent (39%), representing sixty-seven percent (67%) of the schools, a statistically reliable and very high return for a mailed questionnaire.

Presidents and deans were most widely represented in the survey with response rates of forty-eight percent (48%) and forty-seven percent (47%), respectively, while faculty had the lowest response rate at twenty-five percent (25%). Table 1 shows the response rates for all positions.

Table 1

President	48%
Dean	47%
Registrar	45%
Librarian	44%
Board Chairperson	33%
Student leader	31%
Faculty leader	25%

In order to ensure that the sample was unbiased, that is, that those responding to the questionnaire accurately reflected the entire group surveyed, the attributes of the 131 schools that responded to the questionnaire were compared to those of all 195 ATS member, associate, or candidate schools. Factors used for comparison were region, denomination, enrollment size, university affiliation, membership in a consortium, and degree of affiliation with ATS.

Table 2 shows a comparison of "expected number" of schools within each attribute to the actual number responding. The "expected number" of schools in each category was calculated by multiplying the percent of all 195 schools with a certain attribute by 131 (the number of schools represented in the

3

Table 2
Response to Questionnaire
(Expected vs. Actual Number of Responses)

Region	E	A	Denomination	E	A	Enrollment	E	A	University Affiliated	E	A	Member Consort.*	E	A	Status w/ATS	E	A
Canada	15	11	ABC.	3	4	0-99:	34	31	Yes:	11	8	Yes:	54	59	Accred.	112	113
New Eng.	9	10	CCDC.	3	3	100-199:	44	48	No:	120	123	No:	77	72	Cand.	6	4
Mid. East	25	25	INTD.	17	19	200-299:	18	20		131	131		131	131	Assoc.	13	14
S. East	19	21	LUTH.	7	8	300+	34	32								131	131
Gr. Lakes	28	29	PRESB.	7	9	**130	131										
Plains	12	11	EPISC.	6	6												
S. West	9	13	R.C.	36	32												
Far West	13	11	S.B.C.	4	2												
**130	131		UCC.	5	6												
			UCCAN.	3	3												
			UMC.	9	8												
			OTHER	31	31												
				131	131												

*Listed as a member of a consortium in ATS Directory
**Not equal to 131 due to rounding

4

sample). Using "enrollment" as an example: if the enrollment of the 131 sample schools exactly reflected that of all seminaries and schools of theology, then of those responding twenty-six percent (26%) would have an enrollment of less than one hundred; thirty-four percent (34%) would have an enrollment between one hundred and 199, fourteen percent (14%) would have an enrollment between two hundred and 299, and twenty-six percent (26%) would have three hundred students or more. The "expected number" would result in thirty-four, forty-four, eighteen, and thirty-four schools respectively. In actuality, the 131 schools that responded to the survey had a distribution of thirty-one, forty-eight, twenty, and thirty-two for the four enrollment categories. In other words, smaller size schools (with enrollments of less than one hundred) were slightly underrepresented and medium size schools (with enrollments from one hundred to 299) were slightly overrepresented in the survey. It is evident from this example, and the analysis of other factors, that the response to the survey is representative of theological education in general.

To complement the standardized data collected through the survey, the research team conducted a series of personal interviews with 198 people, selected from more than sixty organizations in eleven cities. Sites were selected to represent a cross section of seminaries and schools of theology on the basis of five criteria:

1) region--all eight regions as defined by ATS were represented in the site visits;

2) denominational affiliation--sites were selected to represent a variety of denominations overall and to investigate combinations of denominations in one location;

3) ethnic or racial population--sites were selected to represent diverse populations overall;

4) modes of cooperation--based on research of catalogs and through initial interviews, sites were selected to include consortia with a university affiliation which were listed in the ATS directory, consortia without a university affiliation which were listed in the ATS directory, clusters of schools where no formal consortium existed, and varied community and professional affiliations; and

5

5) status of cooperation--sites where the formal consortia were said to be experiencing difficulty or said to be successful were chosen.

At each site team members attempted to identify persons in a variety of institutional positions and representing a variety of perspectives. The team sought to talk to persons at each school of theology at the site and persons holding different positions at each school, such as CEO, academic dean, faculty, trustees, librarian, students, and staff. The team also talked to the cluster leadership and staff at all locations where formal consortia were in place.

The following attitudinal perspectives were sought in developing a list of interviewees:

1) committed positive users, true believers in the cooperative ventures;
2) neutral or nominal participants;
3) skeptics;
4) individuals with a historic perspective on the cooperative venture;
5) individuals who had been instrumental in shaping the cooperative venture;
6) individuals fairly new to the venture; and
7) individuals who had experienced cooperation at different locations.

In areas where a formal consortium existed, the team contacted the executive officer of the consortium to generate an initial listing of names. Where no consortium existed, the team contacted CEOs and faculty at schools directly.

Questions asked interviewees covered their personal history and activities at the seminary, the form of cooperation at their school, the governance and objective of the effort, sources of support and opposition, the benefits, problems and future of cooperation. Interviews were conducted after the questionnaire responses were received, so researchers had an initial framework from which to work at each site. Interviewees were assured that their individual responses would be shared only with the research team. Most interviews were conducted by a single interviewer although several included two interviewers. Care was also taken to assure the interviewee that this was not an evaluation 'per se' of the consortium or cooperative arrangements. The team was interested in experiences of cooperation, not in determining whether a venture should be funded or not.

6

Each site was visited by two of the researchers over a period of two or three days. Interviewing in pairs enabled researchers to cross check and reconsider initial impressions on site and to investigate other aspects of the situation. The team mitigated the problem of inconsistency of technique and interpretation by rotating partners at each of the sites. Each interviewer was thus able to compare methods and conclusions with several different colleagues.

Using a combination of a closed, more objective survey instrument with a more subjective, open-ended interview technique strengthened both the breadth and depth of the study. Although the questionnaire allowed the use of comparable and generalizable data, the respondent had little opportunity to explain the meaning or reasons for his or her responses. Interviews, on the other hand, could not be as easily generalized across all responses since they covered different material from one interview to the next. However, interviews enabled the interviewees to interpret and nuance their responses and allowed a deeper understanding of the topic at hand.

B. The Concept of Cooperation

To assess the recent history of cooperative ventures and understand the strategic role they might play in the future of theological education, the study team searched for concepts of cooperation that would help leaders in theological education and potential donors evaluate a broad array of cooperative activities and identify possible directions for the next five to seven years.

An early phase of the study included a preliminary set of interviews with leaders to determine the kind of boundaries the researchers should set for the types of cooperation to be examined. Each interviewee delivered the same message: define cooperation in the broadest terms possible and allow to emerge the rich range of collaborative experiences and activities that have taken place in theological education.

In its search for broad concepts of cooperation, the team turned to the work of three theorists who have explored notions of cooperation, especially within an organizational context.

Chester Barnard, in his classic work, *The Functions of the Executive* , defines an organization as a "system of cooperative activities". [2] His definition focuses on the formal, "consciously coordinated" functions of an organization, rather than on the informal exchanges among people within an organization.

Carl Joachim Friedrich, in contrast to Barnard, defines the organization as "all arrangements working together". [3] Within this broad framework, he considers both voluntary and enforced interactions. In his view, organizations can be grouped according to at least two dominant "styles", cooperative or coercive. Cooperation designates situations in which persons work together voluntarily and for their mutual benefit. Coercive or directive organizations are those in which the contributions of the members or participants are ordered and enforced. While he notes that it is rare for an organization to be purely of one type or the other, the distinction is an important one, which allows insights into different organizational styles or cultures and limits the possibility of overextending the definition of cooperation.

Robert Axelrod examines the notion of cooperation in relation to voluntary action and to the presence or absence of a central authority or other enforcement mechanism. [4] He applies his theory of cooperation to complex organizational settings as well as to the interplay between two individuals. Through empirical research he has sought to identify the conditions under which essentially self-seeking individuals or agencies can develop cooperative relationships without a central authority to police their actions.

Axelrod's theory of cooperation and his empirical findings provided the team with a broad framework within which to consider and assess the wide range of cooperative ventures in theological education. His research suggests the following points which became guidelines for the team's analysis of its findings:

1) Cooperation can be initiated by just a small cluster of individuals who are prepared to reciprocate, even in settings where no one else will cooperate.

2) For such cooperation to take place, at least a small portion of these individuals' interactions must be with each other and must have certain minimal characteristics. Specifically, there must be some clustering (not necessarily spatial) of individuals who:
   a. are the first to cooperate or are open to the possibility of cooperation;
   b. are able to distinguish between those who respond to cooperation and those who do not.

3) It need not be assumed that the individuals or agencies involved are

rational or that they engage in a means-end calculus.

4) Participants do not have to exchange messages or commitments. The evolutionary character of cooperation allows cooperative ventures to succeed even if the participants do not know why or how they cooperate.

5) Trust or altruism among the participants need not be assumed. By first cooperating and then using reciprocity — responding in kind to whatever the other player did in a previous move — defections from the cooperative venture will appear unproductive and collaboration will be maintained. Cooperation does require that an individual or agency be able to recognize another actor who has been dealt with previously and remember the nature of that interaction so that subsequent actions might be responsive.

6) There is no need to assume a central authority or any other characteristic of a formal organizational setting for cooperation to take place. Coercion is not essential. Cooperation based on reciprocity can be self-policing.

7) For cooperation to be stable and enduring, the future must have a sufficiently large shadow, that is, the possibility and importance of a next encounter among the participants must be great enough to make deception now seem unprofitable and somehow undesirable. This also requires participants to recognize that they have a significant enough chance of "meeting" or interacting again.

With this conceptual framework in mind, the study team was encouraged to think not only in terms of major clusters or consortia but also in terms of informal arrangements, temporary alliances and less structured types of cooperative activities. The team was reminded of a conclusion reached by the Resource Planning Commission during the 1960s:

> There will be no single model by which it will be possible to describe the structural or even functional linkages which will unite their [seminaries'] cooperative endeavors.[5]

9

It is this broader view of cooperation which the team used to examine and assess cooperative ventures in theological education during the past twenty years.

C. Structure of The Report

This document represents the final report of the Cheswick team, a cooperative effort among five team members, which stands now as a collective contribution. The team's hope is that this report will strengthen cooperative ventures in North American theological education.

The structure of the report is as follows: Chapter I above has provided an introduction to the research methods and theoretical underpinnings of the study. Chapter II provides a brief overview of the evolution of cooperation in theological education. Special attention is given to the consortia movement of the 1960s and 1970s. Chapter III describes the major findings that emerged from the questionnaire survey and the interviews conducted in the United States and Canada. It reports on the wide variety of cooperative undertakings which exist in theological education as it is practiced in the mid-1980s. Finally, Chapter IV concludes with recommendations based on the findings of the research. The appendices include: I) The Questionnaires, and II) List of Persons Interviewed.

Notes for Chapter I

1. See Jackson W. Carroll, "Project Transition: An Assessment of ATS Programs and Services," *Theological Education* 18 (Autumn 1981): 45-165.

2. (Cambridge: Harvard University Press, 1938), 75.

3. (New York: McGraw-Hill, 1963), 126-130.

4. *The Evolution of Cooperation* (New York: Basic Books, 1984).

5. "Resources Planning in Theological Education," *Theological Education* , Vol. 4 (Summer 1968):791-792.

II. THE EVOLUTION OF COOPERATION

A. Early Developments in Cooperation

1. The Development of Cooperation among Protestant Seminaries

The first Protestant theological seminary in North America was founded
by New England Trinitarian Congregationalists at Andover, Massachusetts, in
1808. The idea of a three-year, post-college, theological seminary quickly
spread among Protestant denominations and the establishment of other institutions followed in rapid succession. Presbyterians established Princeton, Dutch
Reformed created New Brunswick in 1812, Episcopalians founded General
Theological Seminary in New York in 1817, and Unitarians organized
Harvard Divinity School in 1819. As Natalie Naylor has persuasively argued,
"Within a generation of the founding of the first seminary at Andover in 1808,
the theological seminary on the Andover model was the norm among
Congregational, Presbyterian, Episcopal and Reformed denominations."[1]

Almost immediately, along with the new seminaries, came some forms of
cooperation. The American Education Society (AES), founded in 1815, gener-
ated greatly needed funds for the new schools through the creation of scholarships for seminary students. Because of its financial base, the society was also
the moving force in establishing uniform standards among the emerging institutions. Seminary leaders from Andover and Yale were the primary motiva-
tors behind the organization, but nearly every Protestant seminary in the country was in touch with the AES.

The AES was highly successful in seeking the establishment of the
three-year, post-B.A. degree institution because of its powerful funding prac-
tices. The AES granted substantial scholarships to seminarians but insisted
that the institutions in which the seminarians were enrolled fit the Andover
model. Because of its policies, the AES became the nineteenth century's primary accrediting agency for Protestant theological seminaries. Schools of a
wide variety of theological persuasions received funds, but none which did not
conform structurally. It was hardly a form of mutually agreed upon cooperation, but the existence of the AES did facilitate contact among Protestant theological seminaries in the United States, almost from the time they were first
founded. [2]

In the second half of the nineteenth century, the ideal of a theological seminary continued to gain strength in nearly all American Protestant denominations. With the decline of the American Education Society by the time of the Civil War, there was no single organization to ensure uniformity or cooperation among the diverse schools, but seminaries continued an informal exchange of information, accepted students from other schools and usually shared a common understanding of goals and structures.

In the last decade of the nineteenth century and the first of the twentieth, the split between the liberal and evangelical wings of Protestantism grew with significant impact on the world of theological education. Seminaries became increasingly aligned with one camp or the other. During these same years, conferences were occasionally held between the leaders of seminaries of the same denomination such as the Conference of Congregational Seminaries or the meetings of the Baptist Theological Faculties Union. At such gatherings new ideas could be shared, new methods evaluated, and common problems discussed in a friendly atmosphere.

From its founding in 1903 into the 1920s, the Religious Education Association's Department of Theological Seminaries provided the principle means for the exchange of information and ideas among seminary leaders at least within the liberal wing of Protestantism. It represented the development of an informal means of cooperation among the representatives of the larger and more prosperous seminaries such as Union (New York), The Divinity School of The University of Chicago, Yale, Hartford, Princeton, and Harvard. Whether or not anyone envisioned the REA functioning as an accrediting agency, many hoped that it might become the center of a seminary system based on mutual cooperation and consensus.[3]

Two important studies of American Protestant theological education in the 1920s and 1930s, the first conducted by Robert L. Kelly in 1922 and the second conducted by William Adams Brown and Mark A. May from 1929 to 1934, were instrumental in expanding the level of cooperation. [4] These reports led directly to the decision by the informal Conference of Theological Seminaries, which had been founded in 1918, to hire an executive director. This step, taken in 1934, the same year as the publication of the Brown-May report, began the process of transformation into a full-fledged accrediting agency . In 1936, when the conference changed its name to the American Association of Theological Schools in the United States and Canada (AATS), it became the actual accrediting agency for North American Protestant schools of theology.

14

The pattern of mutual consultation would grow with the century, and the association which was founded would certainly act as one of the most aggressive supporters of cooperative efforts in the years to follow. Support for cooperation was not, however, high on the agenda of the AATS or its members for the first quarter century of its existence. Only much later would the organization play a direct role in fostering cooperative ventures among seminaries. From the beginning, however, the existence of the AATS guaranteed a growing level of communication between seminary leaders and greater clarity about the norms on which North American Protestant theological education would be organized.

2. The Development of Roman Catholic Seminaries [5]

The arrival of four Sulpician priests from France in 1791 to open St. Mary's in Baltimore was the starting point of Catholic seminary education in the United States. In 1808 the Sulpicians opened a minor or preparatory seminary to train boys in humanities and piety as preparation for theological studies for their seminary. This institution, Mount Saint Mary's College at Emmitsburg, Maryland, was ceded to a corporation of diocesan priests who introduced theological instruction for seminarians. To support themselves, the seminarians in turn taught college boys. A kind of "cooperative venture" characterized this early Roman Catholic seminary experience, that is, one in which seminary training was combined with a lay college.

In the early nineteenth century, bishops sent their seminarians to Baltimore and Emmitsburg, but twenty-two dioceses had been established and some bishops founded their own seminaries. Most of these local seminaries collapsed during the 1840s and 1850s due to one of several reasons: lack of seminarians, lack of personnel to conduct them, and lack of regular funding to sustain their operation. From the 1840s through the 1870s some forty new dioceses were formed, but only a few local seminaries were started. Four dioceses were promoted to the rank of archdiocese, with neighboring dioceses grouped around them to form ecclesiastical provinces. Efforts were made to form a regional seminary in each province, an example of cooperation by necessity, since the smaller schools could not be sustained. These freestanding seminaries were labeled "total institutions" whose internal life was ordered for the training of priests.

This was not the only model for American seminaries. Communities of priests also sponsored schools for laymen and seminary training on the same grounds. At the Third Plenary Council of Baltimore in 1884, bishops looked to the future development of an American clergy trained along standard lines for all seminaries and issued seminary decrees aimed to improve the content and length of seminary training.

Another kind of cooperation took place around The Catholic University of America, opened in 1889 with a pontifical charter from Pope Leo XIII. It had a special role in stimulating interest in improving seminary programs. Some smaller orders opened houses of study near the University so that members could attend the University's theology program. The network of free-standing seminaries and houses of study in the neighborhood of Catholic University is the closest manifestation of a larger cooperation among Catholic seminaries in the nineteenth century.

In the early twentieth century the separation of seminary communities from lay culture was more complete and the self-contained world of the free-standing seminary came under the more rigorous standards decreed by church authority. The lines of authority in the church were vertical: from the seminary officials to the bishop to Roman authorities in the case of diocesan seminaries; in religious orders, from the seminary officials to the local religious superior to the international superior to Roman authorities. There was no provision for horizontal interaction among seminary educators. Roman authority with its concern for universal standards of its own normally took no cognizance of the need for seminary educators to interact among themselves or to relate seminaries to local education standards. This pattern continued until the seminary reform of the 1950s, which is described in a section below.

B. Developments in the Last Four Decades

1. The Chicago Cluster

The decision in the early 1940s to form the Federated Theological Faculty of the University of Chicago happened quite apart from any AATS involvement. The Federated Faculty was created in 1943 when a new dean at the Divinity School of the University of Chicago proposed to Disciples Divinity House, Meadville Seminary (Unitarian), and Chicago Theological Seminary that a joint, university-related faculty be created to supervise both the professional Bachelor of Divinity degree and doctoral level work. The

16

Federated Faculty was an exciting idea and also the belated fulfillment of William Rainey Harper's dream for the University of Chicago in the 1890s as the hub for a series of denominational divinity houses which, in cooperation with his new university, would provide a more comprehensive pattern of theological training than was currently available.

Nevertheless, from the outset there were serious problems. The relationships between the different member schools, and between the schools and the University were never clear. More important, there was little fundamental agreement on the educational philosophy or purpose of the new entity. A series of internal reorganizations failed to confront the basic tension between those who saw the orientation as primarily towards being a graduate school of the University and those who were primarily committed to excellence in the training of ministers. Finally by 1959 all of the parties were willing to agree that the federation should be ended and the schools went their own ways, each negotiating its own cooperative arrangements with the University.[6]

With the ending of the Chicago experiment at the beginning of the 1960s, it became an example of the potential issues awaiting future cooperative arrangements. Those in the 1960s who wanted cooperation always assured their audience that they were avoiding the Chicago mistakes. Those who opposed it had only to use the words "Federated Faculty."

2. Niebuhr, Williams, Gustafson Report

Symbolic of the lack of interest in cooperative ventures among seminaries in the 1950s is the famed Niebuhr, Williams, Gustafson report. Their report, *The Study of Theological Education in the United States and Canada*, does not mention the idea of cooperation. Yet that report, written between 1954 and 1957, is the starting point for research on theological education in this half of the decade. Comprehensive in its scope and content, written in an era that pre-dates the turmoil and rapid change that would characterize future decades, it exists as a bench mark in the memory of some of those who provide leadership for theological education today. Indeed, the Resources Planning Commission initiated its 1968 report with the question "Has anything really changed since the Niebuhr report came out?"

The first volume by Richard H. Niebuhr, *The Purpose of the Church and Its Ministry*, described the emerging concept of the minister as pastoral director, and defined the theological school as the intellectual center of church life.

It advocated that the study of theology be viewed as a kind of ministry and that there be a dialogue in seminary between theology and other church activities.

The second part of the report, *The Advancement of Theological Education*, focused on recent trends. The study emphasized the need for able theological teachers as the key problem in theological education. It suggested that faculties see themselves too much as individuals and not enough as collectives who examine the "wholes of meaning and effectiveness of common work". The study focused on internal dynamics and did not address external operations. It did propose a reorganization of seminary curriculum including a lengthening of the course of study to four years. Most observers at the time agreed, however, that this proposal involved financial resources which were simply not available.[7]

3. New Cooperative Ventures

Despite some of the issues that surfaced with the Federated Faculty in Chicago and the lack of interest in cooperation in the major seminary study of the 1950s, cooperative efforts in theological education did expand during the early years of the 1960s. Black seminaries in Atlanta, like white schools in Chicago, had a history of association dating back to the 1930s. Part of the impetus for the decision to form an Atlanta cluster came from a foundation, the Rockefeller Sealantic Fund, which in 1955 rejected an application from Methodist Gammon Theological Seminary because it was a denominational school. At the same time the directors of the Fund made it clear that a cooperative venture in Atlanta would receive funding. After an initial study, the Interdenominational Theological Center (ITC) was chartered in 1958 as a cooperative effort of four schools of theology each serving primarily Black students with four different denominational bases. It began operations in 1959. The ITC avoided many of the tensions of the Chicago experience. It had a clear purpose and mandate: the education of Black ministers for American churches, especially in the historically Black denominations. And although relationships were developed with colleges in the Atlanta area, there was no one dominant university divinity school to intrude on cooperative efforts.[8]

A second major center for cooperation in theological education emerged in the 1960s in Berkeley, California. There had been conversations for some time about cooperation among San Francisco area seminaries, but the first decisive action came when the Church Divinity School of the Pacific (Episcopal) issued an invitation to any seminary ready for immediate action to join with them. This invitation by-passed the vetoes of those schools which had resisted the idea and provided the basis for a union which others might join. The result of this move was The Graduate Theological Union (GTU) which began as a cooperative venture on the doctoral level among several seminaries whose primary focus was B.D. work but which also desired graduate programs. Its work was greatly strengthened by the development of close cooperation with the University of California, Berkeley. The presence of a major state university provided a fruitful setting for ecumenical cooperation in which no divinity school or denomination exercised special control or felt excluded from the program.[9]

After their initial incorporation as The Graduate Theological Union in 1962, the original four Protestant seminaries (Baptist, Episcopal, Lutheran, and Presbyterian) were joined by the interdenominational Pacific School of Religion(1964), and by Dominican (1964), Unitarian (1964), Jesuit (1966) and Franciscan (1968) schools. [10] According to several observers interviewed in this study, the addition of Roman Catholic schools secured the future of the GTU. As several persons reported to the study team, "Protestants tend to cooperate better with each other in the presence of Catholics."

Other clusters also appeared in the 1960s. In Dubuque, Iowa, the faculty of Aquinas Institute of Theology (Dominican) had begun conversations with their colleagues at the Theological Seminary of the University of Dubuque (United Presbyterian) and Wartburg Theological Seminary (American Lutheran Church), which led in time to the formation of the Association of Theological Faculties in Iowa.[11]

In Canada, the Toronto Graduate School of Theological Studies was incorporated in 1964 by four Protestant theological seminaries which had been cooperating for two decades and were joined two years later by a Roman Catholic school. Finally, in 1968 the Boston Theological Institute was organized, eventually including nine schools, Protestant, Roman Catholic, and Orthodox, the only consortia including an accredited Orthodox school, which cooperates through cross-registration and the sharing of resources.[12]

4. The Resources Planning Commission

The founding of these early cooperative arrangements among seminaries was far from the only development of the early 1960s. Shortly after the final publication of the Niebuhr report, a new decade ushered in a whirlwind of change in the United States which was to affect the seminary scene in North America.

The 1960s was a decade which experienced the explosion of diverse points of view and values. The beginning of the decade saw the rise of the civil rights movement; the end saw the emergence of the women's movement. For three years (1962-1965) the world experienced the Roman Catholic Church's attempt to throw open its windows in 'aggiornamento' through the Second Vatican Council called by Pope John XXIII. During the same years, Protestants in the United States began their own cautious steps towards greater cooperation beginning with the "Blake-Pike Proposal" which led to the formation of the Consultation on Church Union (COCU) by several of the major Protestant bodies in the United States. Thus for both Catholics and Protestants, ecumenism took on an importance not previously considered. Overshadowing everything else, however, the entire decade was fraught with the growing awareness and protest over the United States involvement in Viet Nam. Respect for authorities and confidence in the stability of institutions was shaken in all parts of the nation's life. The United States experienced the assassination of a president, and, five years later, the murder of civil rights leader Martin Luther King, Jr., and candidate for the presidential nomination Robert F. Kennedy.

In this same year, 1968, the Resources Planning Commission (RPC) of the Association of Theological Schools (ATS, formerly AATS), which had been appointed two years earlier, issued its report. This document attempted to read the signs of the times and respond with suggestions to meet the changing needs for ministry preparation and the challenges thought to face seminaries in the 1970s.[13]

The events of the 1960s were integral to the challenges facing seminaries and their preparation for ministers. The RPC report emerged out of the winds of not only cultural change but also changes emerging in theological education itself. These changes in theological education can be characterized as a) a new emphasis on a professional model of preparation for ministry, b) emergence of an ecumenical drive that motivated theological networking on new levels, c) a new awareness of and commitment to ministries related to social justice concerns, especially urban ministry, and d) a modeling of inter-institutional cooperation in clusters or consortia. A brief account of these dimensions

20

follows.

a. Professional Education

In 1966 Charles R. Feilding published *Education For Ministry*, a study on practical training for ministry with special emphasis on supervision.[14] Jesse H. Ziegler, the executive director of ATS since 1960, had already begun to incorporate the concept of professional education for ministry into considerations for seminary education.[15] An emphasis on professional education dominates the book and is the context for the issues of supervision and field education, the use of seminars and the case study method, internships, and Clinical Pastoral Education.[16] Feilding noted that the faculties of many institutions accepted corporate responsibility for professional education, a plea that had come from the Niebuhr report. The very nature of this method of education would require seminaries to seek cooperative arrangements for field placements.

b. Vatican II and the Ecumenical Drive

In the 1950s, Roman Catholic seminary educators began to think about and seek accreditation from regional accrediting bodies. Reformers were greatly encouraged in their efforts by the words of Pope Pius XII in the apostolic exhortation, *Menti Nostrae* (1950), that seminary courses in the liberal arts should not be inferior to those in the equivalent secular institutions. Seminary educators began to develop among themselves a sense of common concerns, initially through educational conferences of various religious orders that sponsored their own seminaries or were engaged in seminary education for dioceses. Here the need for reform was discussed, and common educational policies within a religious order's institutions were formulated. The forum for seminary educators nationally became the seminary department of the National Catholic Educational Association. In 1958 the Association appointed a full-time executive for the seminary department, Rev. J. Cyril Dukehart, who was a persistent advocate of ways of bringing the seminary out of its isolation from the rest of the educational world which often regarded the Catholic seminary as inferior. He targeted three major areas for seminary reform: first, the importance of accreditation so that unordained former seminary students and clerical alumni would have academic records and degrees recognized in

21

the educational world; second, the formation of an American Association of Catholic Theological Seminaries as a means of improving the standards of seminaries and establishing a professional degree for seminaries; third, the acute problem of the weakness of over 100 minor and major seminaries with fewer than fifty students. Many seminary educators shared Dukehart's vision of the needs of the Catholic seminaries. They held regional meetings to discuss these ideas. The Middle West was especially important because of the relationship that seminary educators there formed with the North Central Association of Colleges and Universities to advance accreditation for degrees for theological studies.

By 1962, the year of the opening of the Second Vatican Council, the main lines of an agenda of seminary reform in the United States in a burgeoning system were determined. The following decade saw the implementation of most reforms that were designed to end the isolation of the seminary and to enlarge its educational purposes. These changes were accompanied by two occurrences: theological renewal brought by the Second Vatican Council that would alter the content of seminary learning; and rapid cultural changes taking place within the American Catholic community that would change the attitude of young men toward entering the seminary.[17]

The impetus of Vatican II and the openness of Protestant seminaries also led to broader ecumenical networks among institutions of theological education. Formal cooperation was facilitated by the acceptance of Roman Catholic seminaries as members of the Association of Theological Schools. The influx of Roman Catholic seminaries into ATS began in 1966 when Maryknoll, Mount St. Alphonsus, Weston, and Woodstock were accepted as members.[18] By this time, ecumenical motivation became an assumption of theological education in a way that would have not been possible only a few years earlier.

While these membership trends were occurring among Roman Catholic seminaries, ecumenical trends could also be seen elsewhere. For example, the Episcopalian report by Nathan M. Pusey and Charles L. Taylor, *Ministry For Tomorrow*, which was published in 1967, concludes, "Where is the kind of theological education we have been advocating most likely to take place? A clear case can be made for an urban location, near a university, with opportunity for ecumenical cooperation with other seminaries." [19] These recommendations were to parallel those of the RPC.

Vatican II also began a trend which RPC did not foresee, a widening of the horizon for ministry. The Vatican Council asserted that the mission of the church belonged to all Christians, not only the hierarchy. As a result, thousands of Roman Catholic men and women, members of religious communities and not, began to identify their work as ministries or to seek new work which would become their ministry. Thomas O'Meara refers to this phenomenon as "the explosion of ministry" and states:

> The United States was soon filled with open seminaries,
> universities, theological schools and summer programs ed-
> ucating thousands for ministry. By mid-1970s, it was clear
> that in the United States (Protestant churches were moving
> more hesitantly) Roman Catholicism was conducting a
> dual system in theological and pastoral education, and both
> tracts could not escape the milieu of wider ministry.[20]

Partly because the majority of Protestant seminaries had accepted a small number of women for some time, Protestant seminaries and churches did not seem to experience the same sort of change in the numbers and kinds of people considering themselves ministers during these years. Later in the decade, however, the percentage of seminary students who were women would expand rapidly, from a tiny minority to the majority of the student population in some schools. Within Catholicism, however, parishes and other ministerial settings such as hospitals, prisons, and church social agencies were soon staffed in whole or in part by persons who were not ordained but who were qualified for the ministry. The Roman Catholic seminary was only one of several settings in which these skills were gained.

c. Social Justice

From the early 1960s the civil rights movement caught the attention of seminarians as no single movement had for more than a decade. William J. Schneider's description of the response at Episcopal Theological School in Cambridge, MA (ETS) to the march from Selma to Montgomery in March 1965, is indicative of scenes throughout the middle years of the decade: "It appealed to their sense of social justice, and a number immediately responded. The questions "Are you going?" and "Are you coming with us?" were repeatedly asked as students passed one another in the halls or visited in the dormitories." [21]

23

That particular march recruited Jonathan Daniels from ETS who was shot to death in Haynesville, Alabama, the following August. He became, perhaps, the best symbol of a new generation of seminary students whose commitments to the immediate struggles of the decade were at least as strong as their academic and professional interests.

While Daniels was able to go to Selma in 1965 with the full support of his seminary, students in the mid-sixties were also beginning to question the role of their own institutions in social issues with which they were grappling. As the decade wore on, students at many seminaries were questioning the curriculum, the power relationships within the schools, and the investment holdings of their own institutions. One seminary president described student perceptions of his office: "They probably will think of him as the symbol of the establishment and this is not altogether helpful." [22] It was with all of these tensions in mind that the authors of the RPC penned their study.

d. The Cluster Model

While the work of the RPC was progressing, the consortium model of cooperation among theological institutions had already begun to emerge in a number of places and it became a source for the Commission's inquiry. In the final chapter of its report, the RPC notes it had witnessed the development of The Boston Theological Institute, the re-location of Bexley Hall to Rochester, New York, and northside and southside Chicago projects. Of course the earlier developments, especially regarding graduate programs in Berkeley and Toronto and the cooperative efforts in educating Black ministers in Atlanta, were significant models for the RPC. The report also had high hopes for discussions underway in Philadelphia, which were being conducted in cooperation with the Resources Planning Commission itself. In all, it listed six cities which had all the resources for significant cluster development to take place and eleven metropolitan areas in which there were sufficient resources.

Basing its work on these four major developments in the areas of professional education, ecumenism, social justice, and consortia growth during the decade, the RPC operated on the following assumptions:

- that change in theological education is required and that the rate of change must be accelerated;
- that theological education was now taking place in an ecumenical era

where better relations with churches began by learning together; and
- that theological education was for a pluralistic society.

Its conclusion is summarized in the concept of the central cluster:

The landscape of theological education in North America a
decade hence is likely to be characterized by a small number
of major clusters. These will be in proximity to large universities in the major metropolitan area in which most of the
nation's great public and private universities are now located. We believe that these clusters will be ecumenical in
character... It seems altogether probable and desirable that
these groupings of seminaries will be linked in a great variety of ways; there will be no single model by which it will
be possible to describe the structural or even functional

linkages which will unite their cooperative endeavors. [23]

Although the Commission's vision clearly noted a preference for urban or
metropolitan, university affiliation, and ecumenical emphasis, it should be
noted that the Commission also stated that a center would probably grow up in
a rural area removed from a metropolitan, university setting.

It is also notable that it was not one of the Commission's assumptions that
cooperation would be cost saving. While the authors of the report saw the
cost-savings potential in combining resources, improving student/faculty ra-
tios, avoiding administrative duplication, sharing library costs, and better use
of physical plants, they acknowledged that contractual agreements, tenure and
more professional staff for larger plants would offset these cost-savings.
Savings may be unobtainable or only realized over a protracted period. The
report concluded that seminaries should not expect any significant reduction
in cash outlay as a result of cooperation.[24] Furthermore, it should be added
that the curriculum committee of the commission expected cooperation to
begin at the basic degree level.

The conclusion of the work of the RPC is often referred to as the
Froyd/Laney report. Issued in 1972, it reviewed the "changing character of the
crisis in theological education" which had been identified by the RPC. An
emergent focus in the crisis was finances. The report identified the elements
of the financial crisis as 1) inflation , 2) too much plant, 3) overextension of

program, 4) too many faculty, 5) too few students, and 6) no new sources of income. It urged responses to this crisis through clustering, relocation, or abandoning the traditional seminary model. In place of the latter, it noted possible substitution of a foundation model and/or of continuing the professional education and research paradigm.

The report noted several gains in the development of clusters: the enrichment of faculty from an ecumenical perspective, the creation of some innovative and experimental programs, the possibility of sharing current programs through common calendar, and progress in effective plant management. By this time the significance of library cooperation also had emerged. On the deficit side, problems centered on finances. Not only did clustering not reduce costs but it often brought about new expenses. The hoped-for foundation funds, seemingly easily attracted because the venture was ecumenical and not denominationally based, had not materialized. The report identified major obstacles that consortia struggle with today: lack of cross-registration because of distance, lack of serious ecumenical dialogue, and lack of any serious influence in individual appointment of faculty at member institutions. In general, these factors emphasize the perpetuation of duplicate resources. The report noted a waning enthusiasm for the cluster idea. Several factors were cited: the burden on faculty, students' unawareness, administrators unable to see the relationship of the cluster to the concerns central to their institutions, particularly finances and church-related issues.

The Froyd/Laney report identified some problems inherent in clustering itself. Specifically, the issues involved in the structural question of a consortium are location, redeployment of faculty, freeing other resources, and the issue of church identity. All these issues have remained the struggles of consortia currently in existence. The report tried to envision an alternative beyond clustering — the theological center. The best it could do was to identify the concept of theological center by what it was not:

> It is definitely not a cluster or a consortium, for they will have none of the granular relationships that are so crippling to this kind of organization. Nor is it a federation of schools --there is no disposition to risk the tragedies of the past on this score. Neither is it a merger into an interdenominational school, with the features of a union seminary. [25]

What it *was* remained a mystery. The report was clear on what the Center concept would need to accomplish: "a structure of operation in which the issues of cost reduction can be faced, quality of program given priority, diversity and unity be supported, and openness to the future assured." [26]

5. Charles L. Taylor Report

In 1973, five years after the RPC issued its report, Charles L. Taylor was commissioned to study cooperation in theological institutions in the United States and Canada. [27] The fast pace of change in the 1960s had slowed; all of the major consortia or clusters had been established. One could take a look at how cooperation was progressing. The three areas which shaped his inquiry were 1) the effectiveness of cooperative structures to help students face the urgent problems of the day and to better foster a servant church, 2) the financial problems facing theological institutions, and 3) the structures of cooperation. He wondered how to draw the line between a school's autonomy, integrity, freedom and adherence to tradition, and the relinquishment of some of its functions. He found approval for cooperative ventures from the administrator, student, and faculty, although students found obstacles to cross-registration and faculty worried about over-commitment and loss of turf. He characterized three weaknesses in cooperation: 1) fear of loss of freedom when one school is dominant and another weak, 2) programs in cooperation that are window-dressing and not at the heart of the seminary enterprise, and 3) institutions and faculty that are out to protect their own.

Taylor sensed structural problems over the proper role of seminaries in relation to each other. In regard to costs, he found a common complaint that cooperative functions add to already overstressed budgets without corresponding savings or gain. He noted a high expectation that cooperation would produce savings, in spite of the warnings in the original RPC report that this was not likely. He also noted that clusters reflect the weaknesses of their component parts. In summary, he concluded, "If initial expectations have in some cases not been fulfilled, one reason may have been unrealistic expectations and neglect of hard facts of economic inflation coupled with ecclesiastical recession." Essentially the same conclusions were reached as in the Froyd/Laney report the year before but Taylor did not venture the proposal of another type of cooperation.

6. Leon Pacala's Report

In 1980 the executive directorship of the ATS changed and the new director, Leon Pacala, undertook a visitation of 124 seminary campuses at the beginning of his tenure. His findings were reported in *Theological Education* in Autumn, 1981. Pacala summarized a three-fold legacy of the 1970s: an ecclesiastical identity of theological schools, a professional curriculum, and a transformation from a single purpose to a multipurpose institution. In this latter category he noted the rise of the D.Min. degree and the increase in the median age of students and in the number of women. Pacala named identity and institutional concerns as an agenda for the 1980s. The identity issue for the institution is a dynamic played out between the church and the academy.
Institutional concerns constellated around five poles: operational finances vs. capital resources, numbers of students vs. quality of students, faculty considered as a guild vs. a profession, and the academic programs as a theologate vs. theological services. In the latter category, he noted the centrality of the M.Div. program even though the percentage of student enrollment in this basic degree is declining.

Finally, Pacala described the cooperative dimension of theological education as a struggle between self-sufficiency and dependency. In talking with CEOs he found the prevalent belief that cooperative ventures were important in principle. Yet, also prevalent was the notion that they were expendable, only nominally significant, and that the programs of the individual seminaries would be little affected if existing structures were to disappear. The CEOs found significant areas of cooperation in faculty and curricular enhancement.

7. Project 2000

The final report of a study on theological libraries, begun in July 1981, was published in 1984. [28] It is of interest to this study because of the integral way in which cooperation is considered in library planning and the directions for the future which are indicated by the library specialists consulted in Project 2000. The purpose of Project 2000 was to analyze the roles of theological libraries for the remaining years of the 20th century, identify the resources needed, and propose strategies, programs, and guidelines to assist development, implementation, and evaluation. The emphasis in library development had been on uniformity and, while helpful in some ways, this homogenizing effect had also weakened libraries. The report therefore turned to the affirmation of diversity and cooperation. Reliance on computer systems and central bibliographic resources have established the fact of cooperation. The next task is to harness effective library cooperation to achieve goals of continued planning of library services, preservation of diverse collections, and broadening of collections through internationalizing them. Other future goals outlined in the report were "an enlarged partnership between ATS and theological librarians", greater coordination of development without thwarting local initiative, and the encouragement of the concept of all North American libraries as one collective resource.

An analysis of the results of a survey on libraries conducted as part of the Project 2000 study showed that of the schools surveyed, sixty eight percent (68%) were involved in one or more cooperative arrangements and seventy-one percent (71%) of cooperative library programs were part of a more comprehensive cooperative structure. Librarians have preferred programs which were voluntary, but fifty percent (50%) of those schools which anticipate entering into arrangements note that the new agreements will be more structured and involve greater financial commitments. The two strongest reasons for cooperating were access to other collections which had strengths and expansion which was possible when collections are developed jointly. Of the libraries involved with cooperative programs thirty-two percent (32%) would find the dissolution of their primary cooperation very detrimental and fifty-five percent (55%) moderately detrimental. Libraries cooperating with schools which offer Ph.D./Th.D. programs were more likely to view the loss of cooperation as very detrimental.

8. The Expansion of the Locus of Theological Education

The diversity of church-related ministries exercised by different people — who are professional, non-ordained, salaried or volunteer — raises an issue of where and how these ministers are educated. Seminaries are no longer thought of as the only institutions which train ministers. For example, in the Roman Catholic community, universities and colleges have established successful, permanent, pastoral institutes and programs for the unordained minister or for further education of the ordained minister. One could ask if this emerging multi-locus of the theological enterprise augers a crisis of identity for the seminary and raises the issue of the seminary's future in an increasingly competitive and entrepreneurial market. It also surfaces an important question for this report: who must be included in the discussion of cooperative enterprises?

Cooperation among seminaries has clearly been a factor in North American theological education for all of this century. It emerged as a major concern of both the schools and the funding agencies during the turbulent 1960s. Because of this historic context, discussions of cooperative ventures in theological education usually revolve around the model which emerged during those years, a model clearly defined by the three factors of university connections, emphasis on urban ministry, and ecumenical awareness. In spite of the pleas within the most significant documents of cooperative planning for avoiding a single rigid model, the remembered ideal has become, for many, quite rigid indeed. At the same time, both the theological ferment and the actual practice of seminary cooperation in the 1980s provides a picture of much greater diversity. It is that contemporary picture to which this report now turns.

Notes for Chapter II

1. Natalie Ann Naylor, "The American Educational Society, 1815-1860," unpublished Ed.D. dissertation, Teachers College, Columbia University, 1971.

2. See Naylor for an excellent analysis of the American Education Society.

3. For a critical review of the role of REA in theological education, see William Douglas MacKenzie. "The Standardization of Theological Education", *Religious Education* 6 (1911): 253-261.

4. Robert L. Kelly, *Theological Education in America: A Study of One Hundred Sixty-One Theological Schools in the United States and Canada* (New York: George H. Doran, 1924); William Adams Brown and Mark A. May, *The Education of American Ministers*, 4 vols (New York: Institute of Social and Religious Research, 1934); see also a memorandum written by Barbara Wheeler, "The Movement toward Cluster, Consortium, and Centers in Theological Education: A Review of the Movement in the Past Decade and Some Notes toward the Formation of Policy", c. 1975-76 on file at Lilly Endowment.

5. This entire section is condensed from "How the Seminary Developed" by Joseph M. White. Publication forthcoming in monograph form.

6. Aute L. Carr, "The Federated Theological Faculty of the University of Chicago: An Analysis of the Agreements, Structures, and Relationships, 1943-60," *Theological Education* 4, Supplement 1 (Summer, 1968 1): 61-64.

7. H. Richard Niebuhr, Daniel Day Williams, and James M. Gustafson, *The Study of Theological Education in the United States and Canada*, in 4 vols., *The Advancement of Theological Education, Reflections on the Aims of Theological Education, The Purpose of the Church and its Ministry*, and *The Ministry in Historical* Perspectives (New York; Harper & Row, 1954-1957).

8. Aute L. Carr "The Interdenominational Theological Center: A Descriptive-Evaluative Study," Theological Education 4 Supplement 1 (Summer 1968.): 33-36.

9. David S. Schuller, "Graduate Theological Union: A Descriptive- Evaluative Study," *Theological Education* 4, Supplement, (Summer 1968): 4-7.

10. The Graduate Theological Union, *Catalog,1983-1984/ 1984-85*, 28.

11. David S. Schuller, "The Association of Theological Faculties in Iowa (Dubuque): A Descriptive-Evaluative Study," *Theological Education* 4, Supplement 1 (Summer 1968): 22-32.

12. David S. Schuller, "The Toronto Graduate School of Theological Studies: A Descriptive-Evaluative Study," *Theological Education* 4, Supplement 1 (Summer 1968): 47-60.

13. The report, "Resources Planning in Theological Education" *Theological Education* 4 (Summer 1968) :751-844 was supplemented by three documents: "Theological Curriculum for the 1970s" , *Theological Education* 4 (Spring 1968) :671-745, "Cooperative Structures for *Theological Education*", *Theological Education* 4, Supplement 1 (Summer 1968): 1-80, and

"Economics and Organization of Theological Education" *Theological Education* 4 Supplement 2 (Summer 1968) :1-89.

14. (Dayton: AATS, 1966); The Feilding report was funded by the Lilly Endowment. Feilding was assisted by Thomas Klink, John Minter, and James Glasse.

15. Jesse H. Ziegler. *The Association of Theological Schools Through Two Decades: Reflections on Theological Education*, 1960-1980, 1984.

16. Feilding, 112, 119, 148-149, 184-185.

17. Much of the discussion of Catholic seminary development in this section is based upon the work of Joseph M. White, "How the Seminary Developed".

18. Ziegler, 198-200.

19. (New York: Seabury Press, 1967), p. 125.

20. Thomas Franklin O'Meara, *Theology of Ministry* (New York: Paulist Press, 1983), p. 10.

21. William J. Schneider, ed., *The Jon Daniels Story* (New York: The Seabury Press, 1967), 25-26; much of the material in this section is based on "The Triumph of the Seminary," an unpublished paper from Auburn Theological Seminary's History of Reform in American Protestant Theological Education project, ca. 1977.

22. John C. Bennett, "Comments on 'The Office of the Presidency'," *Theological Education* 6 (Summer 1970): 304.

23. "Resources Planning in Theological Education." 791-79.

24. Ibid, , 804-810.

25. See American Association of Theological Schools in the United States and Canada, 1972 Biennial Meeting, p. 73.

26. Ibid.

27. "Cooperation in Theological Education in the U.S. and Canada", *Theological Education* 10 (Autumn 1973) :3-38.

28. Stephen L. Peterson, "Theological Libraries for the Twenty-first Century: Project 2000 Final Report," *Theological Education*, 20 (Supplement 1984) :7-114.

III. FINDINGS:
CURRENT EXPERIENCE
AND
ISSUES CENTRAL TO COOPERATIVE VENTURES

The major sources for data in this section are the 514 questionnaires that were returned by seminary leaders and a series of in-depth interviews conducted by the team with 198 leaders in theological education in eleven cities in the United States and Canada. Issues central to the discussion of cooperation in theological education can be grouped into three basic areas:

A. The current experience with cooperative ventures

B. A set of factors which leads to what is usually perceived as successful cooperation

C. A number of issues that need further consideration. These factors, which influence cooperation, either have not surfaced in literature before or need special consideration.

Before beginning the account of the findings, the study team wishes to note a general tenor which characterized its experience both in the survey and in the field. The team found variety, vitality, and a willingness of many leaders in theological education to respond to questionnaires and to engage in discussions with the interviewers. And while there was a frankness among many of the interviewees as they identified unease, tension, or conflict, there was also considerable excitement about the many different kinds of cooperation that are currently taking place.

A. Varieties and Value of Cooperation

1. Results of the Survey

The results of both the questionnaires and the site visits provide strong evidence of the variety of cooperative ventures in theological education. In Part I of the questionnaires, the respondents were asked to name the types of cooperation in which their institution participates. Based on a review of literature, definitions of seven different types of cooperation were furnished and respondents were asked to choose among them. An extra open-ended category was also provided. The types of cooperation were as follows:

1. Multipurpose Consortium
2. Single purpose Consortium
3. Informal Cooperation
4. Corporate Rearrangement
5. Joint Research Center
6. Cooperation with Schools of the Same Denomination
7. Cooperation with Nonacademic Institutions
8. Other

A multipurpose consortium was defined as a formal arrangement which results in several types of ongoing joint activities such as academic cooperation, cross registration, shared services or shared facilities. Consortia listed in the directory of the Association of Theological Schools (ATS) would be included in this category as would affiliation with a university or other academic institutions, where cooperation on a wide range of activities can be found.

The definition of a single purpose consortium was limited to institutions that have some formal arrangement covering a single line of activity, such as library cooperation, faculty exchange, shared degree program or field education, to name a few.

Informal cooperative arrangements referred to departments, faculty members, student organizations or administrative staff linked on an 'ad hoc' basis.

Corporate rearrangement meant a permanent change of the governing structure of the institution. Merger would be a typical case.

Joint research center referred to a type of cooperation between two institutions which is specifically focused on an area of research.

A sixth category defined an institution's cooperative arrangements with other seminaries or academic institutions of the same denomination or religion. These cooperative ventures could be multipurpose, single purpose, or informal as well.

The next category defined cooperation with nonacademic institutions such as churches, denominational entities or community organizations. A final category allowed respondents to describe cooperative arrangements that were distinct from any of the arrangements described previously.

The responses indicate that theological educators have developed many different types of cooperation that far exceed the limited number of categories usually discussed in the literature. In addition, the results suggest that there are many different cooperative configurations even within the same category, and that the schools are cooperating on many fronts. In all, the descriptions of the cooperative ventures submitted by respondents from 131 schools, identify sixty different forms of cooperation. On average, each institution participates in seven different cooperative ventures. Table 3 shows the types of cooperation existing at ten percent (10%) or more of the schools in the order of the most frequent occurrence.

Table 3
Types of Cooperation

QUESTIONNAIRE CATEGORY	SUBCATEGORY	PERCENT OF SCHOOLS
Multipurpose	ATS listed consortium	45
Single Purpose	Library cooperation	42
Nonacademic Institution	Continuing education for lay people	37
Research Center	Joint research center	36
Informal Coop	Among faculty	36
Nonacademic Institution	Denominational entity	32
Nonacademic Institution	Field education site	31
Informal Coop	Ad hoc workshops	31
Corporate	Merger	23
Multipurpose	Other than ATS listed consortium	23
Same Denomination	Multipurpose cooperation	21
Informal Cooperation	Among students	18
Other Coop	Regional library cooperation	16
Nonacademic Institution	Pastoral training center, social justice center	15
Same Denomination	Nondegree program	14
Informal Coop	Many forms	14
Single Purpose	Advanced degree program	13
Multipurpose	Affiliation w/ university	13
Nonacademic Institution	Workshops with local groups, businesses	11
Informal Coop	Among librarians	11
Same Denomination	Faculty exchange/ shared faculty	11
Single purpose	Cross registration	11
Nonacademic Institution	Mission organization	10

Participation in a multipurpose consortium and library cooperation are the most widespread forms of cooperation identified by respondents. Forty-five percent (45%) of the schools in the survey belong to one of the consortia listed in the ATS directory; twenty-three percent (23%) belong to a multipurpose consortium other than an ATS listed consortium, and another twenty-one percent (21%) described multipurpose cooperative ventures with schools of the same denomination. Even though library cooperation is often a part of these multipurpose consortia, another forty-two percent (42%) of the institutions listed library cooperation as a separate, single purpose activity of their institution. A large proportion of the schools also have cooperative arrangements with nonacademic institutions such as with parish-based continuing education programs (cited by thirty-seven percent), with the school's denominational entity (cited by thirty-two percent), or with field placement in community organizations and nonprofit institutions (cited by thirty-one percent). Thirty-six percent (36%) of the schools have a joint research center with other schools of theology and twenty-three percent (23%) have gone through a merger. Finally, the informal cooperative arrangements of faculty and students with their colleagues at other institutions is a form of cooperation that exists at more than one-third of the schools (36%).

In addition to asking the respondents to identify the cooperative ventures in which their institution participates, the questionnaire asked the respondents to select the one or two cooperative ventures that are most important for their institution. Figure 1 shows a breakdown of the ventures considered most important according to the CEOs, deans, and librarians. The solid bars show the percentage of schools in which the CEO identified that cooperation as most significant.[1] Patterned bars indicate the percentages for deans and librarians. Belonging to a multipurpose consortium, whether ATS listed or other, was selected by CEOs as the cooperative arrangement which is most important for the schools participating. Of the fifty-nine schools that are in ATS listed consortia and the thirty schools that are part of other multipurpose consortia, CEOs at sixty-three percent (63%) and thirty-seven percent (37%), respectively, considered multipurpose consortia to be the most important cooperative venture for their school. As can be seen in Figure 1, the rankings of the deans for the most important cooperative ventures closely parallel that of the CEOs. For example, both cite membership in a consortium most frequently. Also important for CEOs and deans are multipurpose cooperation with schools of the

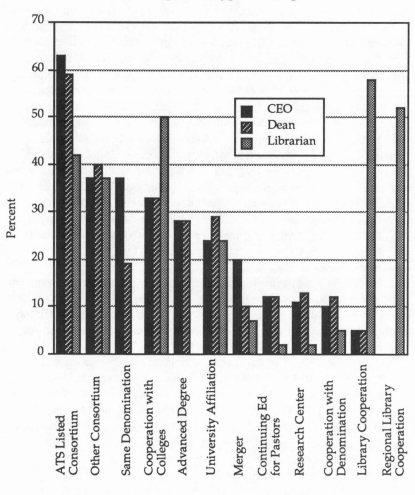

Figure 1
Most Important Types of Cooperation

same denomination and multipurpose cooperation with colleges. Next in importance for CEOs and deans are cooperation in the advanced degree program and affiliation with a university. Of the eighteen schools that have a cooperative advanced degree program, separate from their membership in a consortium, CEOs and deans at twenty-eight percent (28%) identified that as the most important venture. CEOs at twenty-four percent (24%) of the seventeen schools that are affiliated with a university identified that relationship as most important.

Not surprisingly, librarians chose library cooperation as the most important cooperative venture for their schools. Librarians at fifty-eight percent (58%) of the schools that have library cooperation with other seminaries mentioned this inter-seminary venture as most important. As highly ranked by librarians was regional library cooperation, receiving recognition by fifty-two percent (52%). Librarians also mentioned multipurpose cooperation with colleges as an important form of cooperation. Of the twelve schools that have joint programs with colleges, fifty percent (50%) of their librarians claimed such cooperation as important.

Although approximately one-third of the schools surveyed mentioned their participation in cooperative arrangements with nonacademic institutions such as parishes, denominational organizations or field education sites, for the majority of the schools these ventures are not the most important. Similarly, while approximately one-third of the schools mentioned informal arrangements among faculty or 'ad hoc' workshops, these were rarely listed as the most important form of cooperation for the school.

2. Specific Examples of Successful Cooperation

The responses to the questionnaire indicate that different seminaries have found a variety of ways to cooperate based on their own geographic, regional, and denominational needs. The theological education being offered to students in the United States and Canada today is believed to be richer because schools are cooperating in many ways, from inter-library loans or consolidated libraries, to joint seminars and advanced degree programs, to cross-registration, to mutual support among administrators. This remarkable range of activities does not readily fit within a single limited set of categories. For example, regarding the basic multipurpose consortium, it is not a matter of "all or nothing." Rather, the specific needs of particular settings guided the reality of each arrangement.

To learn more about the specific adaptations and to complement the standardized data collected by means of the survey, the research team conducted a series of personal interviews with 198 seminary executives, board members, faculty, staff and students selected from more than sixty institutions in eleven cities. Sites were selected to represent a cross section of seminaries on the basis of five criteria: region, denominational affiliation, ethnic or racial population, modes of cooperation, and status of cooperation. The interview results reveal much about the diversity of cooperative efforts.

• In several locations the consortium of the seminaries has become a strong institution in its own right, coordinating library resources and registration procedures, and awarding, either in its own name or cooperatively with a major university, the research doctorate of the seminaries. In these cases, the consortium has become a relatively well organized structure in which decisions are made through established channels. At the level of the research doctorate and in terms of making library resources available to students and faculty of the constituent schools, these consortia are often cited as having made significant contributions to the academic quality of theological education in North America.

• In other locations, informal, more loosely knit networks among seminaries serve the schools involved. For example, although the name of a consortium may or may not have been adopted in these locations, the dominant characteristics are not unified degree programs, centralized offices, nor integrated physical resources, but rather cooperation around special events. In some settings there are ongoing seminars in which faculty and students from member schools gather to pursue a special topic, or mobile seminars in which participants jointly travel to different sites, sometimes overseas. At times, these informal cooperative ventures involve some cross registration, although geographical distance often limits its extent. Finally, in these kinds of ventures, strong interpersonal relationships and mutual support among the leaders of the institutions become major factors or much discussed features of the cooperative arrangements.

In an economically troubled region of the United States, twenty-five seminaries are cooperating with two undergraduate colleges and a regional religious association to provide a combination of special summer courses for seminarians, winter term work for pastors and lay leaders, supervised internships, and research opportunities for seminary faculty members. By focusing

40

on the special ministry needs as well as the rich religious heritage of the region, this cooperative venture is seeking to strengthen the church's ministry through a unique educational program for persons, lay and ordained, who are engaged in ministry in this region.

• In another part of the country, a single seminary has evolved into a center for reflection on the ministry needs of the region, involving a surprisingly ecumenical student body and faculty in the process. After describing changes at the institution, one president remarked: "I never would have agreed to develop what we now have. It would have been too much of a departure from the past. But one thing at a time came along, and each one made sense." The school now serves students of the local diocese, sponsors programs for a variety of religious orders, both male and female, and offers programs for lay people in both English and Spanish. It also has an informal cooperative program with a seminary of a different denomination in another part of the state so that students of that denomination can pursue the first two-thirds of their M.Div. program closer to home. In addition, all M.Div. graduates of this seminary are required to be able to preach and practice ministry in two languages in order to facilitate ministry in the region.

A local minister spoke of the importance of this seminary as a regional center of reflection on the needs of local ministry. He insisted that there was no way that students traveling to a distant metropolitan area for academic training in a great university center could achieve anything close to the practical exposure to ministry and the opportunity to use this experience as a basis for further theological reflection. The seminary's cooperative outreach has made such opportunities possible in its region.

• In one of the cities that has a long standing pattern of cooperation among the seminaries, a group of women has established a theological center of its own that has a formal relationship to one of the seminaries and whose programs are recognized by nearly all of them. This program provides a year of reflection in feminist theology for a group of women each year who spend time in both theological study and supervised ministry. The program serves those who are seminarians and wish to apply the credits received towards their M.Div. degree, those who are on sabbatical, and those who are evolving their own forms of ministry. Women seeking academic credit in the program may be enrolled either as special students in the M.Div. program of one of the Protestant seminaries in the area or in one of several. program at a local Catholic college.

• A major state university is the host to a commission which "brings together members of eight human service professions to address collaboratively complex ethical and social problems encountered increasingly in professional practice." Begun in 1975, this program includes seminary students and faculty as only one of a number of professional groups who study "issues at both ends of the life span, changing family lifestyles, chemical dependency, and public and private violence." While this program may not fit standard patterns of cooperation in theological education, participants judge it to be most worthwhile. The curricula of several seminaries in the state have been enriched because their students are able to participate in this program, gaining exposure to the work of a wide variety of secular professionals and reflecting on their own ministry in light of this experience.

Among these and many other cooperative ventures, there are some that are long standing and well established and others which are new and may or may not continue. Some fit a familiar model of cooperative ventures in theological education. Others do not. But all appear to strengthen theological education, and may serve as models for similar work elsewhere.

3. Evaluating the Benefits of Cooperation

Part II of the questionnaire asked respondents to identify factors that affected the participation of their institution in cooperative efforts. It asked CEOs and academic deans to identify the motivations for entering into cooperative arrangements; it asked all respondents to identify the benefits and problems of cooperation; it asked all respondents to rate their own level of support for cooperation and the level of support they perceived was given by other members of the institution.

According to the CEOs and deans, the primary motivations for cooperating were a combination of philosophical and practical reasons. Faculty motivation was not surveyed. Table 4 shows the top motivations and benefits of cooperation selected by the CEOs and deans. For the most part the two groups concur. The number one motivating factor was "To provide a stimulating environment for learning." Other important motivations in order of priority were: ecumenism, expanding educational opportunities at minimum cost, and expanding library resources. With the exception of "expanding educational opportunities at minimal cost", the actual benefits reaped from cooperation matched fairly well the expectations of the CEOs and deans.

Table 4
Motivation and Benefits of Cooperation

| | CEO'S | | DEANS | | FACULTY |
	MOTIVATION	BENEFITS	MOTIVATION	BENEFITS	BENEFITS
Provide a stimulating environment for learning	71%	71%	79%	69%	64%
Ecumenism	52%	45%	53%	53%	64%
Expand educational opportunities at minimal cost	51%	38%	53%	46%	-
Expand opportunities for study, research and association	_	_	_	_	55%
Expand library resources	49%	51%	51%	49%	45%
Student/ Faculty Recruiting	25%	30%	29%	22%	27%
Expand programs in geographic areas underserved	21%	18%	22%	20%	17%
Save money	21%	21%	23%	15%	26%
Denomination or church promotes it	21%	13%	15%	9%	-
Field placement opportunities	-	-	-	-	15%
Upgrade skill level of staff	-	-	-	-	13%
Increased opportunities for grants	7%	11%	9%	10%	9%
More efficient administration	-	-	-	-	6%

In the questionnaire, just over fifty percent (50%) of the CEOs and deans mentioned "expanding educational opportunities at minimal cost" in the questionnaire as a motivating factor in cooperating, while only thirty-eight percent (38%) of the CEOs saw this as an actual benefit of their cooperative efforts. Since the question includes two aspects: 1) expanding educational opportunities and 2) at minimal cost, it is not clear which of their expectations were unmet.

The additional library resources and increased opportunities for grants were the only two areas where perceived benefits moderately exceeded expectations. It is noteworthy that library cooperation, identified by approximately fifty percent (50%) of the CEOs and deans as both a motivation and benefit, was a relatively marginal benefit in the view of the original Resource Planning Commission proposals. This is perhaps because university libraries were seen as more significant resources than all the seminary libraries. Today, library cooperation has come to be very important — the glue for some consortia and a valuable part of cooperation in most areas — even where cooperation on other matters is not significant.

The questionnaire also asked respondents to compare their own levels of support for cooperative ventures with that of their colleagues and others in their institution. Table 5 shows the perceived level of support for cooperation measured on a scale of 1 to 5, ranging from "strongly opposes" to "strongly supports" cooperation. The level of support for cooperation attributed to people in the institution is fairly high with mean values all exceeding 4.0. In other words, CEOs, deans, faculty, and board members indicated that everyone in their institution supports cooperation. When comparing the relative strength of the support, in most cases, the respondents said that they are more supportive of cooperation than their colleagues at the same institution. For example, on average the CEOs gave themselves a 4.79 rating of support compared to a low of 4.11 for their denomination and a middle level of 4.37 for their governing board.

44

Table 5
Level of Support

RESPONDENTS

	CEOS	DEANS	FACULTY	BOARD
YOURSELF	**4.79**	**4.78**	**4.66**	4.65
FACULTY	4.45	4.46	4.33	4.71
RELIGIOUS ORDER	4.53	4.38	4.13	4.63
GOVERNING BOARD	4.37	4.39	4.22	4.43
BISHOPS	4.23	4.19	4.45	4.61
STUDENTS	4.14	<u>4.10</u>	4.02	4.52
DENOMINATION	<u>4.11</u>	4.21	<u>3.97</u>	<u>4.11</u>
MEAN	4.37	4.37	4.26	4.52
STANDARD DEVIATION	.24	.23	.25	.20

SCALE: 0= N.A.
1= Strongly Oppose
2= Oppose
3=Indifferent
4= Support
5= Strongly Support

KEY: **high support**= more than 1 S.D. above the mean
middle support= within 1 S. D. of the mean
<u>low support</u>= more than 1 S.D. below the mean

Again the perception of the CEOs and deans closely resemble each other. After themselves, each group sees faculty, religious orders (where applicable), and governing bodies as more supportive of cooperation. Students and the denomination as a whole are perceived as less supportive than are the other groups. Bishops (where applicable) fell in between. The statistic about denominations might be evidence in support of findings in the site interviews. When a seminary is perceived as closely controlled by a bishop or denominational body, this perception may cause theological educators to be more cautious about initiating a cooperative venture.

B. Factors in Successful Cooperation

Up to this point, the results of the questionnaire and the interviews reported have indicated the variety of cooperative ventures in theological education and how leaders in the field measure some of the benefits achieved. To pursue the question of evaluation further, this inquiry needs to distinguish between successful forms of cooperation and unsuccessful forms. Among these forms, which ones should be fostered and encouraged, which ones not?

It became clear to the research team that theological educators often judge the success of cooperative ventures in terms of a single model: the multipurpose, "world class potential" consortium located adjacent to, or affiliated with, a university, such as found in Toronto and Berkeley. Anything and everything else is judged by many people in the theological arena as something less, not just something different. Interviews reveal that accompanying the judgment voiced by theological educators is a considerable amount of guilt, sense of failure, disappointment; of lost opportunity, of pride, defensiveness; of resistance to the dominant model, or of envy, depending upon who is doing the evaluation and from what vantage point. As noted throughout Section A above, there is a remarkable and diverse array of cooperative activity that goes on both in and outside of consortia. With the exception of a few keen or perhaps partisan respondents, most leaders in the field tend to measure these accomplishments against much larger expectations of what could be or should have been.

The purpose of this inquiry is not to define a single model of successful cooperation against which all ventures should be measured. Rather the goal is to identify critical factors that together lead to measures of success in cooperative undertakings in theological education. The factors are:

- Appropriate leadership for the venture
- Respect for the basic identity of the cooperating components
- Absence of a premier seminary, which is often a university school. This means no single entity is in a position to dominate and no one institution or group fears domination by others.
- Tacit or specific agreement not to interfere with the M.Div. curriculum of any institution
- Ecumenism
- Attention paid to logistical realities, that is, geographical proximity, time and staffing issues, and scheduling.

1. Leadership Issues

a. Founders and Early Leaders

The founders and early leaders of the cooperative venture played a significant role in the formation, shape, and vitality of the ventures. At several locations a charismatic leader or leaders were mentioned as the ones who provided the impetus for cooperation and were responsible for putting the initial design in place. In one major consortium several of those interviewed referred to the "genius" of a single founder who apparently had both the vision of the kind of cooperation that would emerge and the political skills to lobby the necessary changes through the various faculties and boards of directors. Often these leaders are now retiring or moving out of the picture. There is concern that educators who struggled for years to build trust and a common understanding are now being replaced by new leaders who may or may not share the vision and commitment of their predecessors.

Of course, the need for a new generation of leaders to assume responsibility for cooperative ventures is inevitable. The change can be quite healthy — for example, in settings where the need is to institutionalize arrangements that may have initially depended on the informal agreements or charisma of a few founders. In several cases informal arrangements have become the precursors of more extensive involvement. However, some new leaders have in mind different directions that veer from the course set by those who built a consortium from the beginning. The continuation or legitimacy of cooperation may be in jeopardy if compatible new directions are not found.

While the influence of some leaders was essential to the success of cooperation in some locations, in other cases the action of some educators have produced negative results. In one metropolitan area, some influential leaders have been able to prevent a consortium from developing. One leader opposed cooperation from the beginning. The competition between two charismatic educators, both trying to construct cooperation with a slightly different model, also was cited as an obstacle to building a program. In this instance, both were replaced by other administrators who did not value cooperative ventures and the impetus for cooperation waned.

b. Current Leadership and Management

The role and structure of current leadership is strongly influential in the continuation or cessation of cooperative efforts. The way services are rendered, both in terms of who leads and what roles they have, varies from place to place. The length of service, the power of individuals, and the tasks which leaders are assigned, all make a difference in the operation of consortia. Based on field visits, some observations about the ways current leaders fulfill the management function are detailed below.

The services of persons who direct consortium activities or execute decisions of a consortium can be purchased, rented, or volunteered. When services are purchased, a person is hired to do the work of a director. This person is often not affiliated with any member institution. When services are rented, the person contributing the services does so upon the agreement of the member institution to which she or he belongs. Release time from one job is given, so that work compensated by the consortium may be taken on. When the services are volunteered, they come from persons in member institutions who do the tasks of direction in addition to their tasks in the member institution. These individuals may or may not have release time from duties within their own school.

Whatever form consortium leadership takes, it is influenced by the top level management in the member institutions. The rapid turnover among CEOs of seminaries makes it difficult for new leaders to absorb the intricacies of leadership in their own schools, let alone within the consortium. As some interviewees noted, "the revolving door of seminary leadership" does take its toll on some cooperative ventures, particularly those that are dependent on oral commitments and personal relationships rather than on institutionalized procedures and formal structures.

The administrative development of some seminaries, particularly the separation and strengthening of the roles of president and dean (or in some cases rector or other titles), and the resulting increase in bureaucracy, presents a new challenge to cooperative ventures. These officials are more influenced by external constituencies on the board, by potential donors, and in denominations by churches or religious sponsors. Faculty, on the other hand, are more likely to be influenced by their respective professional associations and their concern with their immediate teaching responsibilities. The differing perspectives can lead to conflicting views on the value of cooperation or of what sort of cooperative ventures should be pursued.

It takes time for trust to build among member institutions and where distrust is found, cooperation can deteriorate. The discovery of several "end plays" of one CEO has led others to distrust him and to question the viability of doing anything meaningful in the cooperative forum. On the other hand, the opportunity for CEOs to come together is one of the benefits of cooperation which may in fact be fostering a new type of leadership style. One Catholic seminary president reported his surprise and delight at discovering that the president of a conservative Protestant seminary in his consortium shared many of the same difficulties in finding himself caught between the growing liberalism of the faculty and the demands of the denomination. Such connections build trust for further endeavors, while also providing an important kind of support for leaders who may feel quite isolated in their home institution.

It also takes time for trust to build between the CEOs of member institutions and a hired director. One director mentioned that his title and job description changed during his tenure. This change came about as trust was built up and as administrators of member institutions determined what they wanted this person to do. On the other hand, distrust of a hired director can create tension. In three locations administrators of member institutions perceived the directors of the consortia to be using the consortium to build a separate power base and a competing new institution. In one instance, faculty commented that the consortium staffing structure and expenses created an image of "opulence" that enhanced the consortium but did not pay back the institution for what it was contributing. These faculty thought the money put in a director and an office was money taken from salary increases and benefits for them. In another instance, the director was perceived as partisan, not working for the whole. In all these instances, when the term of the director ended, the person was not replaced by rather hiring someone else but by renting someone's time or acquiring volunteer services. Many times this was accompanied by a scaling back of the tasks of the consortium. These latter methods were deemed adequate, especially given the distrust of the model of the hired director.

The role of leadership in a consortium changes through time for a variety of reasons. Perhaps because of frequent change in individual institutional leadership, consortia and clusters have experienced many shifts in design for the position descriptions of persons designated to direct or execute cooperative activities. In some cases, the original purpose and underlying vision of cooperation have become lost in a sea of details. These flow from the complexity of the daily task of administering cooperative activities, which can include elaborate consultative processes, negotiated agreements, and representative committee structures. It is not so much that the purpose and vision have faded, but rather that the types of tasks and number of people involved have become more complex.

The type of leader who is successful in some places may be different from those in another setting. Leadership does not always have to be charismatic to be beneficial to a consortium. Indeed, the study team found instances of an overly charismatic leader becoming such a threat to the leaders of member schools that the cooperative efforts were undercut. At the same time, it has been a requirement of all consortium leaders to date that they have sufficient strength of personality and ability to deal with vague lines of accountability and that they can hold together a structure that often can be fragile or tenuous. Even under such circumstances some persons make excellent contributions as maintenance people, administering prudently a structure that is already in place. However, changing elements in the cooperative pattern or new issues appearing on the horizon may create problems if no new vision is created to integrate the factors.

c. Vision, Commitment, and Priorities

While some observers predicted that the study team would find a declining interest in cooperative ventures among the current generation of seminary leaders, the research team was impressed by the willingness of seminary leaders to discuss these issues, to dream about what the future might look like, and to think through the current reality. This willingness represents an untapped level of commitment to the future of cooperation that should be fostered.

At the same time, there is a sense of isolation many leaders feel in their commitment. At one consortium the leaders of three schools proposed the same expansion of the consortium, and then voiced the belief that they were alone among the member presidents in supporting such developments. Clearly the day to day work of administering a bulky bureaucratic mechanism undercuts the vision that leaders are able to express when they are together.

Still, in many places, the vision and commitment are present when the right opportunity is available for tapping into them. In the late 1960s, the proposals coming from the ATS, along with a national interest in the needs of the cities and in ecumenism provided the right opportunity, and a variety of endeavors flourished. With the right leadership, and the right occasions, such developments could emerge again, although perhaps with a quite different focus and structure.

2. The Issue of Identity

If one looks at the history of theological education in this country, the issue of identity has been fundamental to the founding and maintenance of theological seminaries. In the eighteenth century, a unified Presbyterian church had no school for teaching its ministers. Once it divided into two hostile factions, each founded its own school to ensure its own definition of orthodoxy and to give a point of focus to its movement.[2] Ever since, theological seminaries have been seen as essential in giving identity to a particular denomination, region, or faction, and receiving loyalty from its constituents to the degree that it accomplishes this goal. One student told an interviewer, "I never considered another seminary. I grew up in this state, and people from this state in my denomination go to this seminary." Or as the same school's president said, "Our financial base is dependent on people who 'love the Lord and our denomination in this region.' " Yet this basic issue of identity has too often been ignored or misunderstood by those attempting to do strategic planning for schools of theology, especially in the area of cooperative endeavors.

For an outside observer, there certainly seems to be something repetitive about three schools, within easy walking distance of each other, each maintaining a program in Old Testament, New Testament, Church History, and other disciplines. The result, too often, is a series of programs, all underutilized, and draining away the resources that could be used for one excellent program. However, when one looks at the internal dynamics of the individual schools, and at their supporting constituencies, a very different picture emerges. The ability of each school to stand on its own is an essential element in the sense of identity that generates support. Too often the issue of identity has been overlooked in the discussion of what constituted a reasonable way for seminaries to cooperate.

As the study team further explored this issue in the seminaries, it found that the identity of an individual institution was manifested in several realms: denominational and theological identity, and affiliational identity. Each of these affects the limits and scope of cooperative activities.

a. Denominational and Theological Identity

Cooperation among seminaries is affected by denominational or theological identity. Schools with more in common obviously have an easier time cooperating. However, what schools have in common may be loyalty to a denomination or to a certain stance on a liberal-conservative spectrum.

In some seminaries, identity is seen in terms of theology, a factor that affects cooperation both within and among denominations. It can be one reason why some institutions do cooperate and why others prefer not to cooperate. In the survey, thirty-seven percent (37%) of the CEOs who responded to the questionnaire cited "lack of shared mission" as a factor hindering cooperation. Within denominations, differences in theological viewpoint may be the reason two institutions exist in the first place, as with the Presbyterian schools two hundred years ago. Between different denominations, schools sometimes cooperate if they share a common theological framework, and will refuse to cooperate if they do not. Thus a student reported the great sense of risk involved in moving from one seminary to another of the same denomination with a significantly different theological stance.

In the case of one consortium, an important element in its cohesiveness is the fact that, to a far higher degree than other cooperative ventures studied, it represents one wing of the American church--Protestant and Catholic. There are no evangelical Protestant schools here. The nearby evangelical seminary is completely autonomous, and indeed cooperates far less than its sister schools do in other parts of the country. Other evangelical schools in the state also have no ties to this consortium nor does the seminary for the nearby archdiocese. The primary Catholic involvement is through the seminaries of three men's religious orders, although the bishop of one of the local Roman Catholic dioceses is also a supporter of the venture.

More often than not a strong or characteristic theology is not claimed by a school. Once a school is actually in existence, survival usually dictates appealing to as wide an audience as possible. The experience which Lawrence Cremin describes in the case of the founding of Princeton in the 1740s remains true to the present. The school was founded to serve as a bastion of theological orthodoxy as defined by one wing of American Presbyterianism, but the need to maintain that institution, once founded, "transformed the character of the projected institution by opening admission to adherents of all denominations, by dedicating it to the education of men aiming to be useful in other learned professions, as well as in the ministry, and by moderating the emphasis of its theological curriculum."[3] Seminary and consortia founders in subsequent generations have found themselves with the same problem. Institutions need students, and students bring a diversity unplanned for at the time of founding.

Most people interviewed described themselves as moderate or liberal people who have to struggle in cooperative ventures with colleagues they usually considered as more conservative than themselves. Problems in cooperation were often attributed to these "more conservative" colleagues. Yet few labeled themselves as among the "more conservative" group.

Most interviewees felt that the liberal/evangelical split in Protestantism is now at a point where little competition remains. People do not consider the other viewpoint as an alternative. Given the "acceptance" of the split, institutional identities have become stronger and theology is less an obstacle to cooperation. It is less of a threat to cooperate if a school is secure in its own identity. As the president of a seminary known as part of the liberal wing of his denomination remarked: "We are no longer in competition with the seminary of the conservative wing of our denomination in our region. We may be in competition with liberal seminaries in other parts of the country, but students do not consider both schools in the same state as alternatives to each other. Thus we are free to cooperate more, because we risk less in terms of prospective students or donors."

As reported in interviews, ecumenism is perceived by some as the concern of the liberal wing of mainstream denominations and of less interest to conservatives. One faculty member summed it up, "Conservativism has its chilling effects." For example, in one situation, the conservative reputation of the local Catholic bishop affects the reputation of all institutions of that church, including its seminaries. Those interviewed cited this influence as one of the barriers to cooperation in that region. In another situation, administrators felt that constraints imposed on one seminary in the area by denominational leaders inhibited further cooperation among all the seminaries.

Comments during interviews showed that a significant number of the self-described conservatives valued ecumenism as long as it included respect for their own positions. These interviewees also noted that hesitation to cooperate can be present in liberal institutions, too. In places where a conservative theology is explicit, positive feelings about cooperation often exist, but extensive, formal, cooperative programs do not always flourish beyond the denomination.

When cooperation extends beyond denominational lines, outside observers or some of the participants may judge it as limited or non-substantial. But other participants view it as a positive step and all that can be done at the time. The particular theological perspective of the ministerial education is an overriding concern, echoed by most interviewees, whether self-declared liberals or conservatives. Cooperative ecumenical programs can be secondary to the communication of the theological perspective or, in the case of great theological diversity within the cooperative venture, the program can be viewed as an obstacle to communication of an orthodox theological perspective.

In these situations, the questions of "How much cooperation is appropriate?" and "Who judges the levels of appropriateness?" arise. For example, in one region, the perception exists among participants that there is genuine warmth and mutual support among the different denominations and more cooperation is not needed. One dean reported, "If foundations or accrediting agencies push for more formal cooperation, it would destroy the cooperation we do have."

The denominational issue has grown in significance in this decade. While it is widely believed that evangelical and conservative Roman Catholic seminaries have a strong emphasis on denominational identity and less opportunity for institutional autonomy, other schools accustomed to independence from churches describe a renewed sense that "seminaries are seminaries of the churches" and "they exist for the needs of the churches."

Pressures are felt from denominations to have more programs for their own ministers, such as continuing education and parish-related activities. They also feel pressure from many students for a thorough grounding in their own denomination as a means of improving future job opportunities. One dean responded to a question about the decline of cooperative ventures in his area with this reminder: "We live in the era of roots."

Some denominations also contribute major portions of the budget and in these instances, denominations have a great impact. Other denominations have reduced the funding of theological education to the point where the schools are virtually unrelated to the parent body. One CEO noted, "In those schools where the share of denominational funding is below ten percent of the school's budget, with the majority of funds coming from a mix of tuition and individual donors who give directly to the school, the potential for impact from the denominations is gone." On the other hand, "closely held" denominationally sponsored seminaries resist cooperation in which religious standards are perceived as being excluded and academic standards made the main measure of faculty and student performance.

The potential for the merger of seminaries of the same denomination is another factor that affects cooperation. In a major metropolitan area, the presence of several institutions of the same denomination complicated the discussion about cooperation. At different times, three institutions were discussing merger or consolidation with other institutions of their denomination. Eventually two institutions moved out of the area, each merging with another institution of its own denomination. The third never came to an agreement about merger and remains independent. A consortium has not been set up in that metropolitan area.

A strongly held theology or sense of denominational loyalty, then, has the potential to influence cooperation in two opposite ways. In some cases, difference in theology inhibits cooperation; if a school does not want its students and curriculum to be "diluted or tainted" by other theologies, it may remain isolated. This can be true of liberal schools as well as conservative ones. The issue has more to do with a distinct theological perspective than with the content of that theology. In other cases, clearly defined differences and established identities may free schools to cooperate with those who hold another theological stance.

b. Affiliational Identity

While some institutions identify themselves largely in terms of how they define themselves theologically or in terms of how they are defined in relationship to a particular denomination, still others have an identity that is based on affiliation with a university, a consortium, or a racial group.

In the late 1960s and early 1970s, the "model for successful theological education" was to be a consortium of seminaries affiliated with a university. The RPC study which proposed this model was a key motivating factor for several arrangements of that nature. Of course, long before the era of the RPC some seminaries were founded as, and remain, the divinity schools of major universities.

Certainly several consortia remain weak because one or more of their member schools is bound by the calendar and regulations of its parent university. And in the case of one consortium, the fact that three of its constituent schools are each also part of a major university means that such things as a common calendar to facilitate inter-seminary planning and cross-registration are out of the question. In these cases, the most important cooperative arrangement for a school is certainly the university with which it is associated. The university drives the fee structure and the calendar for these seminaries. Changing their calendars to accommodate other seminaries would not be considered. Other kinds of arrangements with the university, including hiring and program policies, affect the ability of the seminary to cooperate with non-university affiliated seminaries.

In situations where tightly integrated seminaries form a consortium, the identity of each institution may be submerged in the union of all the schools. In these instances, cooperation among the schools is essential for their continuation. It may happen that a shared faculty, as well as libraries and other joint facilities, create dependence among the schools that makes the continuation of cooperation a pre-condition for continued existence.

In a few instances, the identity of a school is based on its racial composition. Where these schools exist, a special opportunity for exposure to a more diverse student population and to a broader perspective has been one of the major goals of cooperation. This kind of identity enhances the opportunities of all schools involved in the exchange. Given the reality that theological education in North America remains a mostly white and male dominated enterprise, more attention to these kinds of cooperative ventures is needed. In a nation in which people of color make up a growing part of the population, new ventures will need to be initiated in which the experience of Black, Hispanic, and Asian peoples will be included at the center of cooperative work, not as a marginal institute.

The integrity of an institution involves its internal image. Schools value their autonomy, independence, and freedom to function within a certain range of commitments--theological, denominational, regional. These are issues which interviewers found to be of fundamental value for schools. If cooperation threatens these foundational aspects of the identity of a school, it is not supported. The desire to strengthen the integrity of individual schools is an issue everywhere. Support for cooperation is more likely to materialize if the participating school believes that its own identity will be enhanced or at least not threatened.

When these issues of identity are appropriately taken into account, there is a widespread feeling that cooperation provides something that an institution cannot provide by itself. For smaller institutions, cooperation makes available a much broader spectrum of courses, strengthens libraries, and provides faculty with increased opportunities for interaction with counterparts in their own disciplines. For larger schools, there can also be a net gain because of more diversity and interaction, which is valued by some more than by others.

c. Prestige

Prestige is another identity issue that affects cooperation. Traditionally, prestige has been defined in terms of an illustrious faculty, a select student body, a university affiliation and an urban location. While the definition of "prestige" may change and may vary from one denomination to another at different times, it is still a factor affecting cooperation. Information gleaned from both interviews and questionnaires suggests that it is the middle-range schools that cooperate most successfully, not those commonly identified as highly prestigious nor those whose circumstances and resources are limited.

What considerations about these schools with differing levels of prestige are operative in determining whether or not they will cooperate? When an institution is "premier", it is less likely to engage in cooperative activities because it fears losing prestige by associating with middle-range schools. It speaks a rhetoric of "subsidizing" cooperation, that is, carrying a greater proportion of the burden in cross-registration and demands on faculty and library, even though numbers can prove differently. The members of the prestigious institutions assume, sometimes incorrectly, that there is a drain on their resources because they are "stellar" and everyone would seem to want to gravitate to them if given a chance. An institution that perceives itself as prestigious fears that its participation in cooperation will mean lending prestige to another institution that does not deserve it. Being affiliated with some denominations, for example, may disqualify the institution from being considered prestigious by its very nature, so a premier school would not want that association. The attitude among "premier" schools seems to be that only "weaker" institutions need to rely on cooperation for prestige.

At the other end of the spectrum, when an institution has few of the qualities that would define it as prestigious, it may have little to offer other schools and so is not sought after for cooperative ventures. It may also be too threatened to risk its minimal autonomy by cooperating. Though few of the seminaries surveyed think of themselves as marginal or weak or suggest that they are about to go out of business, others identified schools that they thought were in this category and for that reason were not able to cooperate effectively.

The third group, the middle range schools, most often engages in successful cooperative activities. These schools seem secure enough in their identities and with their constituencies to offer significant contributions to such ventures. One school, for example, may have several outstanding Scripture scholars while another may have an outstanding library collection that provides special resources for students. By sharing the advantages of each school, the whole consortium may benefit. At the same time, they do not fear lending undeserved prestige nor being drained by schools in a less advantageous position. These obstacles, which can lead to lack of cooperation, are not considerations for the stable middle-range schools and so it appears that cooperation works best where several of these schools exist.

4. Focus on Programs Other than the M.Div.

A key characteristic of the RPC report was an emphasis on its M.Div. curriculum. The adoption of the "curriculum for the 70s" which emerged at the same time, and from the same sources as the RPC, was strongly urged. No school in the United States adopted this part of the report. One Canadian seminary has reported a long and successful experience with the "curriculum of the 70s", but other schools did not follow this lead.

The "Curriculum of the 70s" was designed by the Resources Planning Commission as one of its major recommendations. The hope was that a major restructuring of the M.Div. (then B.D.) curriculum would be one of the results of the redeployment of the resources of theological education that would happen through cooperative programming. This change did not happen to any significant degree. On the contrary, cooperative ventures have tended to stay away from the M.Div. and in fact have succeeded to the degree that they avoided this central program of theological education.

The almost forgotten story of one cooperative venture illustrates the problems of a cooperative M.Div. program. In this case, a group of seminaries developed a carefully designed plan of cooperation which included plans for all of the schools to move to a site near a major university, to share resources in a cooperative M.Div. curriculum that would truly reflect ecumenical concerns, and to make a major commitment to urban ministry, a pressing issue in the late 1960s. If this plan had been implemented the seminaries in this area would have virtually merged into a single institution, offering a single M.Div. curriculum. The program would have been affiliated with a major university, focused on the preparation of urban ministers, and have been highly ecumenical in its character. The separate identity of the member schools would have continued in little more than name. As impressive as the plan was, however, its floundering was equally impressive. Few today remember that there ever was such a thing as this proposed cluster. Some of the reasons for its failure were:

— The constituencies of the seminaries had a hard time understanding how their identity would be maintained in the new cooperative M.Div..

— Two of the major seminaries involved represented significantly different factions within the same denomination; and one of these also had, as a major part of its identity, the formation of small-town and rural ministers. To actually move to the city and join the proposed consortium would be to give up both points of identity for this school.

— The relationship to the university was never clear; more than one university was always in the running as the point of focus.

— No Roman Catholic schools were involved in this proposed consortium, thus heightening intra-Protestant differences.

At the other end of the spectrum, a successful cooperative venture where identity was respected, flourished because:

— A major state university offered a neutral base for the venture, welcoming the cooperative programs while having no divinity school of its own to "guard the door".

— The venture was truly ecumenical, including Catholics as well as

Protestants, and including a variety of groups from each so that smaller differences could be muted. One of the deans from this area said, "The founder's genius was to bring in the Catholics from the beginning, giving the venture a truly ecumenical focus."

At the same time, this consortium also succeeded for two other significant reasons:

— It stayed away completely from the M.Div. curriculum of the constituent schools, the heart of the "curriculum for the 70s" of the RPC, and the perceived heart of theological education. Today the visitor is struck with the fact that at the basic degree level, there is far less cooperation, or even mutual knowledge of programs, among schools in this area than in other settings known for a much lower level of cooperation.

— In addition, all of the schools kept very clear symbols of their identity. The majority of the schools were already within close proximity and did not have to leave their facilities. Those that did move established specific, attractive buildings that serve as a physical focus of their activity. Except for the cooperative library, a very significant exception, each of the constituent schools could return tomorrow to complete autonomy with relatively little impact on the M.Div. curriculum. Each school has its own full complement of faculty members in each of the traditional theological disciplines. Thus it is possible for denominational supporters to "love the Lord and the church in their region" and send money and future ministers to one of this consortium's constituent seminaries, confident that there is a school with their own identity ready to receive them.

The basic focus in this consortium is on post-M.Div. education. The unique reality is that this particular consortium is both a cooperative venture of its member schools and a separate school of its own, standing alongside them and offering its own curriculum as the only research doctorate in theology in the area.

Of course one must ask if this exclusion of the M.Div. curriculum from the purview of cooperative ventures is a good thing. In a long-established consortium, three seminary presidents told the interviewers that they believed the time had come for a new, cooperative look at the M.Div. curriculum of the member schools. None of the presidents proposed the development of a unified M.Div., but they did believe that much could be gained by some cooperative planning and reflection regarding the basic preparation for pastoral ministry. Whether or not such a level of cooperation can emerge, in that consortium or elsewhere, will be one of the important questions for the next decade of cooperative work.

5. Ecumenism and Cooperation

Several views on the role and importance of ecumenism were voiced during interviews. At least one major consortium has as its basic purpose the promotion of ecumenical interaction. Some others indicate that ecumenism is on the decline, though there is substantial disagreement over how to detect or interpret evidence demonstrating that decline. A more common view is that while ecumenism may not be the explicit reason for cooperation, it in fact underlies the essential purpose of cooperation. In its origins, ecumenical interaction developed from a long range goal of church unity, a vision that some say must be reclaimed before ecumenical cooperation can flourish.

Those most concerned with ecumenism who are involved in theological education offer some observations about the status of ecumenical cooperation in seminaries. An important concern is the influence of key outsiders, that is, the roles of boards, chapters, or church bodies in determining the amount and type of cooperation. In some instances, these groups support ecumenical endeavors through their denominational policies. For example, the Episcopalian Church of America examines its graduating students on ecumenical issues. In a broader sense, the Roman Catholic Church, through documents and policies arising out of Vatican II, plunged its members into unprecedented interaction with other church bodies. Though, at the present time, this enthusiasm seems to many to be diminishing, it nonetheless irrevocably changed the interdenominational activity of all churches.

In other instances, interdenominational dialogue is minimal because of indifference or opposition. Most frequently cited was the position of many evangelical groups whose focus is more on saving individual souls than on ecclesiological identity. The attitudes of the church leadership are passed on to the administrations and faculties of seminaries, where cooperation for the sake of ecumenism is not at all valued.

Among those who traditionally promoted ecumenism, changes in theological outlook are affecting relationships. Other issues, such as ordination of women and ethical positions, also tend to divide along denominational lines. To the extent that inertia and indifference prevail over the original vision of Church unity, so does ecumenical activity lag in seminaries. The long term effect on cooperation is not yet determined, but most agree that it is by no means the driving force that it had been in the late 1960s.

In its interviews the team found widespread agreement that ecumenism is on the decline, yet substantial disagreement over how to detect or interpret evidence demonstrating that decline. In the survey, thirty-seven percent (37%) of the CEOs focused on lack of a shared mission with the other institutions as an obstacle for cooperation. Twenty-five percent (25%) cited lack of interest. Twenty-three percent (23%) spoke of the liberal/conservative split as limiting cooperation. With further probing in the interviews, however, nearly all respondents provided personal testimony about how cooperative, specifically ecumenical, ventures among seminaries or among part of their membership have had a significant impact on their growth, development or thought. A faculty member at one school who was advocating withdrawal from the local consortium put it this way, "The consortium helped at one stage. We were terribly parochial and needed to open some doors to the outside world. If we pull out now, it won't stop the friendships, and the programs are of quite limited value."

As this statement also indicates, however, there are major obstacles to interinstitutional cooperation among seminaries. For some, as the professor cited above, the need to return to roots — a better understanding of one's own tradition and the world-wide fellowship of one's own denomination--outweighs ecumenical considerations.

6. Logistical Realities and Cooperation

The survey of seminaries identified a number of important obstacles to cooperation among the schools. Logistical realities such as geography, time/staffing limitations, and financial considerations were the major factors discouraging cooperation. The logistical factors were more important in inhibiting cooperation than ideological factors such as denominational differences or liberal vs. conservative orientation. Figure 2 shows the factors discouraging cooperation that were mentioned by the respondents to the questionnaires. Geography was the greatest hindrance to CEOs and students, mentioned by fifty-six percent (56%) and forty-two percent (42%), respectively, of those responding. Deans and faculty also listed geographical location as an important factor discouraging cooperation.

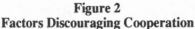

Figure 2
Factors Discouraging Cooperation

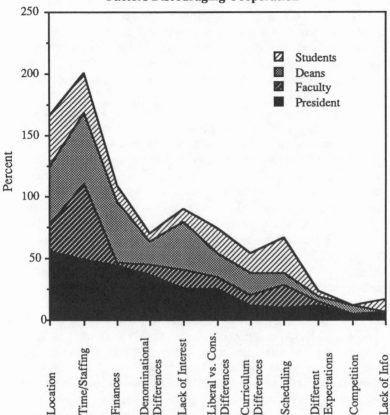

Figure 2 combines the separate charts for presidents, faculty, deans and students into one chart by adding together the percentage of each group citing each factor. The distance between each line and the one below it shows the percentage of that group of respondents citing a certain factor as a hindrance to cooperation. For example, twenty-one percent (21%) of the faculty cited "location" as a limiting factor to cooperation, compared to fifty-six percent (56%) of the presidents. Therefore, the faculty line begins at seventy-seven percent (77%) which is the total of twenty-one percent (21%) and fifty-six (56%). Similarly, the line for deans is added above the faculty and the line for students is added above the deans.

Weather and distance are realities. As one person quipped, "A five minute walk in January in Chicago is a much longer distance than a five minute walk in Berkeley." Such a reality cannot be ignored, however desirable it may be to encourage students and professors to move from one campus to another. Nevertheless the kind of cooperation that is possible when schools are within walking distance of each other, in Berkeley or Chicago, is quite different than when there are many miles, in the case of one consortium almost one thousand miles, between schools.

Conversely, the example of several schools illustrates the importance of geographic proximity to effective cooperation. Study team members observed in several locations that a school moved most of its instructional activities off campus in order to be closer to other schools. Although it retained its campus, the school recognized that in order to be an integral part of the consortium, it must have a presence close to the other cooperating schools.

Many people also spoke of the limitations of time. Time constraints and other responsibilities of staff members was the number one obstacle to cooperation for faculty leaders and academic deans. Figure 2 shows the importance of time to CEOs, faculty, academic deans, and students where forty-nine percent (49%), sixty-two percent (62%), fifty-seven percent (57%) and thirty-three percent (33%), respectively, identified time as a factor discouraging cooperation.

In interviews, students often noted time as a pressure that curtailed their participation in cooperative opportunities. As one said so clearly, "By the time I study for my required courses, take care of my field work responsibilities, and spend a little time with my family, I simply don't have time to take advantage of the programs of other seminaries, no matter how interesting or important they may be." Faculty spoke of similar pressures on their schedules in which cooperation became an add on, one thing too many in an already overly full schedule.

Students and faculty mentioned the problem of incompatible academic calendars as another major factor discouraging cooperation. Cross registration is complicated when courses begin in different weeks or when there are scheduling conflicts with required courses.

7. Financial Resources and Cooperation

The issue of the financial cost of cooperation was also raised by CEOs

and deans as a major hindrance to cooperation, mentioned by forty-four percent (44%) and forty-nine percent (49%) respectively. However, the study
team found that the actual costs and benefits did not lend themselves to exact
calculations. Seminary officials report an increasing level of financial sophis-
tication and expertise but most still find it difficult to measure what they gain
or lose by participating in a particular cooperative activity. Information on
consortium membership fees was readily available. They range from several
hundred to several thousand dollars. However, efforts to agree on how to measure the costs and benefits of cross registration, sharing of faculty resources,
use of facilities, and so on, remain controversial in nearly all locations.

C. Issues for Further Consideration

1. Historical Memory

In spite of pleas for flexibility in the report of the Resources Planning
Commission, the primary result of the report was to fix a very specific norm
of cooperation in the minds of most theological educators who were committed to cooperative ventures among seminaries in the early 1970s. In the popu-
lar memory of the report, the RPC identified a theological consortium as valued and it was defined by three elements: 1) university affiliation as a means
of raising academic standards, 2) urban setting because of the 1960s emphasis
on urban ministry, and 3) ecumenical cooperation, with impetus coming from
both Vatican II and COCU. While the ecumenical goal was, in some ways, the
least significant of the three concerns, it has grown in time to be the dominant
one in the memory of most people.

Given the RPC definition of a consortium, only one or two consortia were
seen as meeting the standard of the day. However, the vision and the pressures
for implementing the RPC plan did lead to a number of cooperative ventures
that were considered partially successful. Finally, a number of schools engaged in some new forms of cooperation, for example, cross-registration,
inter-library loans, special programs/seminars. Some of those involved in
these activities called their ventures a consortium, in part as a response to
pressure on all schools to cooperate. But this was far from the RPC definition
of a "real" consortium, and some schools felt a sense of failure because their
form of cooperation did not more completely fit the model.

65

2. Cooperation Which Is Taken For Granted

Certain forms of collaboration among institutions, faculty, administrators, librarians, and others have become so established, so institutionalized, that they are taken for granted. In such situations, there is less need for an explicit rationale for cooperation. This approach may be desirable, especially where explicit ecumenical effort is no longer able to provide a motivating force. An initial appeal to both ecumenicity and higher academic standard were needed to get a number of schools to share library resources, for example, but once people experience the expanded resources, the arrangement became an institution in its own right. Few now want to or are able to abandon it. The same may be true for certain other kinds of shared resources such as the work of registrars and cross-registration for certain courses.

Studies such as this one, and the reflections they elicit, encourage respondents to focus on that small portion of experience, events, or people, which are remembered negatively, have caused problems or produced tensions — the proverbial ten/ninety problem. The ninety percent that is useful and productive is forgotten, overlooked, undervalued. Although the goals of cooperative ventures are often diffuse, implicit, and unclear, and breakdowns in cooperative arrangements do occur, the team's overall sense is that many of the ecumenical goals of cooperation have been attained. The study of cooperative ventures among theological institutions in North America reveals a breadth, diversity, and richness that should not be forgotten when the tensions and negative dimensions are discussed.

3. Changing Student Demographics

The failure to appreciate the potential impact of anticipated and actual changes in the demography of student and faculty groups on cooperative ventures, and on all of theological education, remains a problem. Several studies by the ATS and others are beginning to point to the changing nature of student populations at seminaries and the changing profile of faculty groups affected by policies on tenure, hiring, and retirement. The population present in seminaries today is quite different from that of twenty years ago. The vast majority of seminarians are not young males, recently out of college, preparing for ministry. The current student body includes a large number of women, the majority at several seminaries, and close to a majority at many more, and considerably older students. At the same time these students are much less willing to travel long distances for their theological education. They bring a much greater diversity of backgrounds to an individual seminary: a variety in age, denomination, sex, and race. At several sites, interviewees discussed these changes with members of the study team. Yet a review of both the interview and questionnaire results showed that few have seriously considered what impact these changes might have on cooperative ventures, such as cross-registration, lecture series, and faculty exchange.

Many schools are attracting older students who have families and community ties which make long distance moves very difficult. Such students are more likely to choose a seminary because of its geographic proximity than its denominational or theological compatibility. In many areas of the country, one seminary will draw from all parts of the spectrum because it is simply in a convenient location. These same students are also reluctant to travel for special events or courses. For a consortium where most of the schools are within walking distance of each other, this may not be an issue but as distances increase, this factor becomes more significant. On the other hand, a single geographically isolated seminary may find itself with a far more diverse student body, with its own in-house "cooperative venture", simply because of location.

Some seminaries may also find themselves increasingly reluctant to make too many demands on students. For the last twenty years seminary enrollments have been artificially inflated, first in the late 1960s and early 1970s by more than a few young men seeking to avoid the military draft for an unpopular war and more recently by the rapid expansion of D.Min. programs which have brought large numbers of older seminary graduates back for a second degree. With the war long over and the D. Min. market reaching saturation, many seminaries may find themselves with plants and faculties much larger than those needed for the number of students seeking admission. Such circumstances are more likely to lead to further competition than cooperation, especially among seminaries who share the same geographic pool of potential candidates.

Notes for Chapter III

1. The percentages were calculated in the following way. The denominator equals the number of schools that participate in each form of cooperation. The numerator equals the number of CEOs, deans, and librarians, respectively who identified that form of cooperation as the first or second most important cooperative venture in their school.

2. James W. Fraser, "The Great Awakening and New Patterns of Presbyterian Theological Education," *Journal of Presbyterian History* 60, no 3 (Fall, 1982): 189-208.

3. Lawrence A. Cremin, *American Education: The Colonial Experience* 1607-1783 (New York: Harper and Row, 1970), 332.

IV. RECOMMENDATIONS AND SUMMARY

A. Synopsis of Recommendations

Both the structure and pattern of cooperation in theological education remain unsettled. While ecumenical and cooperative activities have been established in many theological institutions, and the consortium structure is the dominant model, it would be a mistake to conclude that the pattern of cooperation is set.

Even consortia, whose future five years ago seemed assured, are now experiencing major challenges to their purpose and significant upheavals in their leadership and organization. New problems and new possibilities are emerging. No cooperative venture is immune to what could be called the "configuration" issue. The best way to structure or configure cooperative arrangements seems to be continually under review. The study team believes that uncertainty will continue to characterize cooperative arrangements. The underlying issues are how best to use the resources available for theological education and how to configure networks or systems to accomplish the multiple and diverse goals of theological education. Fragmented responses to these issues both contribute to and reflect uncertainty about cooperative ventures.

Significant regional and denominational diversity in response to the configuration issue adds to the unsettled character of cooperative ventures. Questions of membership, theology, survival, and the potential elimination of valued places, positions, people, purposes, and programs also charge the configuration issue with emotional intensity. Consortia and other cooperative ventures, whose original motivating force may have been ecumenism, personal relationships, the perceived intentions of a donor, the vision of a leader, or the practical interest in a specific task, will continue to affect the potential for re-configuration. What do we want to do, what do we need in order to do it, who should belong or not, and why?

The configuration issue will raise the key question of purpose that all cooperative ventures must face: cooperation for what? Leaders of some consortia and cooperative ventures, as well as association and denominational executives, reported to the study team their efforts to define mission and purpose and set practical objectives for a variety of cooperative activities. There is increasing skepticism about some of the traditional perceptions concerning cooperation such as cost-savings, more efficient use of resources, and

69

ecumenical good will. Resolution of the configuration issues anticipated in the next five years will require more reliable information than most participants in cooperative ventures have been able to produce. The failure to question the model of theological education underlying the Resources Planning Commission efforts in the 1960s will likely be repeated unless "cooperation for what purpose" discussions are focused on the core issues.

In an extrapolation of the data gathered in this study, the members of the research team believe two major developments are needed for the evolution of cooperative ventures.

First, the definition of what constitutes cooperation must be broadened significantly. For historical reasons, cooperation in theological education has come to mean, in the minds of many, conformity to a certain model. While the study team found that variety is the reality in cooperative ventures, the urban, ecumenical, university -related model remains the normative structure. This image limits the vision of many who adhere to it, leading some to a self-complacency and others to a sense of failure to live up to the model. The sense of failure has a double edge. It stifles creativity in developing new models of cooperation that better suit a particular situation or it inhibits a genuine evaluation of a cooperative venture that does not conform to the dominant image. The goal of this recommendation is not to substitute a new structure, but to urge multiplicity. Depending on the purpose and on the opportunities available, many different models of cooperation, some tightly structured, others informally organized, will serve the needs of theological education well. If the goals are set out clearly, if form follows function rather than dictates it, then variety will lead to excellence. And if the definition of excellence is clarified, then there are many ways for cooperative ventures to develop with clearer criteria for success.

Second, discussions of cooperation need to build upon a theological education designed to serve the purposes of the church and its ministry. This recommendation focuses on the goals and not the structures of cooperative ventures in theological education. It leads to three further considerations:
 • a renewed focus on education for ministry, including a commitment to urban and rural ministries, justice ministries, and the ministry of laity as well as clergy. Such a focus will demand a rethinking of the M.Div. curriculum which is at the heart of ministerial education.

• a redefinition of excellence, building especially on the work of recent thinkers who are examining the very nature and development of the enterprise of theology. Such a definition must examine the values which are linked with various theological education traditions, and the values brought to the enterprise by many constituents including people of color, women, and the laity in general. In an age in which mediocrity is accepted in so many areas, the commitment to high academic standards is essential, although it must also be expanded to the point at which excellence includes commitments to justice and beauty as well as rationality, and in which faith is not seen as counter to reason.

• an examination of the evolution of ecumenical spirit which, however much it may have faded in certain quarters, remains an essential element in any theological education because we live in a pluralistic society and in a world which advanced technology brings closer together. Furthermore, Christians have made a commitment to seek unity.

B. Elaboration of the Recommendations

This section outlines a way to broaden the definition of cooperation. It concludes by addressing the question of "Cooperation for what?" and suggests several directions for that discussion.

1. A Wide Variety of Forms of Cooperation Will Serve the Enterprise of Theological Education.

In order to account for the wide variety of cooperative ventures found in theological education, value their diverse contributions, and strengthen efforts at all levels, the study team recommends a distinction between two basic kinds of organizations.

Tightly Linked Systems
• focus on mission and purpose of organization
• invest heavily in written plans designed to achieve specific agreed upon goals
• require continual and constant contact among participants (faculty, students, staff)

71

- tend to develop common or shared resources (buildings, faculty, budgets, endowments, programs, reputation) which require direct central executive authority
- emphasize the significance of the relationships among the members and rely on the permanency of these relationships

Loosely Coupled Systems
- require little agreement about preferences and points of view
- focus on discreet, unrelated events developed through a relatively *ad hoc* process
- allow spontaneous, unpredictable, and discontinuous relationships
- retain separate identities and resources with no central authority
- de-emphasize the significance of the relationship among the members of the system

A complex, highly structured model focuses on what organizations do in terms of mission and planning. Such organizations use an array of rational procedures such as cost-benefit analysis, division of labor, job descriptions, level of authority, specified areas of discretion, and consistent evaluation and reward systems. This is one model of organizational life--and it serves well in some settings. Loosely knit structures also work well in some settings. There are events and aspects of organizations that are intractable to analysis based on rational assumptions; there are organizational relationships that are mutually responsive but which retain their own identity and separateness and may be tacit, or dissolvable, but which also may be the glue that holds organizations together.[1]

The team believes that an examination of a wide variety of possible models for sponsoring cooperative ventures will enable those concerned with cooperation to think in terms of those functions and activities in theological education that can best be served by each approach. For example, loosely knit systems may preserve many independent units which can "know" their environment better. A tightly coupled system has fewer externally constrained elements and is better suited for independent action. Tightly knit systems take advantage of the synergy that arises from ongoing multiple tasks. Informal relationships allow for localized adaptation where preservation of the uniqueness, identity, culture, and separateness of the coupled elements is important.

Loosely knit systems can also be very important when different constituent groups have differing long term goals and senses of purpose, but agree on short term objectives. To build a tightly knit organization would require the submersion of the commitments of the autonomous institutions, something they often cannot and should not do. Less formalized relationships allow a structure to serve an immediate need, while each participant remains quite clear on its differing long-term commitments.

Lack of formal procedures may produce negative results in some settings. Less structured systems find it more difficult to arrive at and carry out uniform changes. They act too slowly, do too little, respond often too late. Authority and accountability get lost when the structure is too informal.

Many existing cooperative activities would be more favorably evaluated and the design of future cooperative activities would proceed more easily if a variety of forms in cooperative relationships were acknowledged. The distinction between tightly knit and loosely coupled systems also allows a combination of approaches to cooperation in a particular setting. Interviewees reported to the team that many of the existing cooperative arrangements include a wide variety of relationships. In one case for example, library cooperation is now in the form of a tightly knit bureaucratic agreement, while the sharing of resources at the M.Div. level is highly informal. In another location, it has been important to keep library cooperation relatively informal, but other parts of the program, such as cross-registration, are more structured. Variety has emerged naturally to fit local needs, resources, and personalities.

The distinction between tightly knit and loosely coupled systems provides concepts which facilitate communication between seminaries and their funding and accrediting agencies. Seminary leaders fear that funding organizations and accrediting agencies do not value the variety of cooperative relationships. Thus the seminary leaders resist renewed interest in cooperative planning advocated by these agencies. Seminary leaders do not want to be forced into a single mold.

2 . The Purpose of the Church and Its Ministry, or Cooperation for What Purpose

The discussion which follows relates to the recommendation that the purpose of the church and its ministry should be the focus in the evaluation of cooperative efforts. It is divided into three areas of concern: a recovery of the commitment to ministry, the establishment of a new definition of excellence, and the commitment to ecumenism.

a. Recovery of the Commitment to Ministry

The central purpose of theological education is the preparation of people for ministry. Yet the study team found that this purpose is easily overlooked in many of the discussions of cooperative ventures. Effective discussion of the purposes of cooperation in theological education requires a recovery of a commitment to ministry. The study team recommends the consideration of at least two issues: the style of education for ministry and the location.

1) The Question of Style

One of the dominant themes of the historical review in Chapter II is the way the definition of ministry has grown in the last twenty years to include large numbers of lay people once not considered ministers, but now very much engaged in ministry and in need of training for their work. Further there is, in many denominations, a growing awareness of the educational needs of all Christians as they recognize the ministerial dimension of their lives regardless of their profession. Thus theological educators are faced with a variety of constituencies: candidates for ordained ministry, candidates for professional ministry who will not be ordained, clergy who desire continuing education or advanced degrees, and lay persons from varying professions who wish an educational experience to examine their vocation as Christians. Often these educational experiences occur within the same institution but exist in separate spheres. The populations of various programs do not interact. Sometimes, different institutions in the same locale handle different populations. For example, a local seminary offers training for candidates for ordination while local colleges or universities have pastoral ministry centers which cater to training for a variety of full-time, unordained ministries. The study team recommends continuing the review of institutional policies which keep the educational experiences of various constituencies separate.

The reality of parishes and congregations is a heterogeneous reality with people who pray together, reflect on the mission of the church, and organize varieties of activities for parish life and action. This variety of people, with varying viewpoints, produces cross-fertilization for reflection and action. Many of those interviewed believed that an educational experience in separate spheres or in separate institutions contributes to a dynamic in which the various constituencies in congregations feel alienation from each other and lack skills in dealing with each other. They stated that a more heterogeneous grouping in theological education could help foster skills necessary for communication in the local setting.

2) The Issue of Location

In an earlier time in theological education, one could assume that students would relocate in order to pursue their studies. Cooperative ventures which focused on centralization of programs and resources relied upon this assumption. The current generation of theological students is older, more settled, and has more responsibilities. Travel to one of a few "centers of excellence" is therefore impossible. For example, a married Catholic woman in Des Moines or a Baptist Sunday School teacher in Memphis will probably not be able to travel to Chicago. Seminaries, and other institutions concerned with theological education, must be committed to the development of local, grass-roots ministers of many types, lay and ordained, in all regions.

The study team believes that options for ministry preparation should be available in local and specific contexts of ministry. Twenty years ago Latin Americans began to argue that sending all candidates for ministry to Europe or North America, or importing the European and North American models of instruction and instructors, did not serve the needs of ministry in their region. Today, church people in many parts of this nation argue that ministers need to be trained locally. For example, a priest in the southwest vigorously asserted that preparation for ministry in the rural southwest with its culture so influenced by that of Mexico, simply could not take place in the great metropolitan centers of the north. The same arguments could be made for other regions.

In effect, these examples suggest a decentralized approach to theological education in the future. Thus cooperation can be either centralized or decentralized. As described in Chapter III, it can occur through a consortium. It can also occur when a small, isolated regional seminary allows itself to become a network for theological excellence for the area, not only for its own denomination, but for others. Cooperation can also be fruitful between seminaries and other non-seminary programs of theological education whether these are located in colleges, lay training institutes, or other kinds of institutions. These ventures may not fit the traditional notion of a centralized consortium, but they represent one of the cutting edges of cooperative ventures in contemporary theological education as it is practiced. Joseph O'Neill's study of semi-

75

nary mergers in the Episcopal Church [2] extends the centralization/ decentralization approach by contrasting centralized planning with a decentralized market type of decision making. The concept of cooperative ventures must be radically expanded so that it can include the marshaling of resources across regional and denominational lines to bring the benefits of first class training to all parts of the continent.

b. Towards a New Definition of Excellence

When the Resources Planning Commission called for a university affiliation for all of the major consortia, and by implication for all seminaries, it did so with the hope that such ties would improve the academic quality of theological education. In the intervening years, many different measures have been proposed to accomplish this goal. A debate has been ongoing between those who would focus theological education primarily on its professional side and those who see a more academic focus. The debate misses the primary reality that the only excellence worthy of the future ministry is one which includes both.

Seminary-university linkages have enhanced the excellence of theological education. Seminaries, by themselves, can become separate worlds isolated from both the life of the church and the scholarship of the larger academic world. Isolation can also be overcome through other kinds of linkages such as those with undergraduate colleges or professional schools in other fields to develop an "interprofessional institute". The study team believes that the goal of excellence in theological education can be achieved through forms of theological education in which no seminary is involved. For example, a college might develop a lay training program which seeks to use a variety of the school's academic resources to serve the continuing education of clergy and lay people, or a group of concerned individuals might develop its own program and find a home for it within a university setting.

Broader opportunities in collaborative efforts among churches, schools, and other groups will lead to a redefinition of excellence in theological education. Certainly all cooperative ventures in theological education need to be supported by high quality teaching and research. But at the same time, any definition of excellence which does not include serious attention to the many constituencies of modern theology cannot be called excellent. Scholarship which does not include the contributions of women, people of color, the poor,

76

is inadequate scholarship. Research methods which focus only on the kinds of documents left by the "winners", by the upper class white males who are often the easiest to document, is incomplete research. Teaching which includes lecturing about a received tradition but does not include the continual process of expanding the tradition is incomplete teaching. Excellence needs to be continually under scrutiny and continually in process of redefinition.

c. Emerging Challenges to the Ministerial Enterprise and to Theological Education

Today, as in every other historical period, the church is confronted with issues in its contemporary scene and is called upon to interpret and re-affirm its mission and ministry. In turn, these challenges shape needs to be met in theological education. As the next decade unfolds, three areas of concern create the horizon for future perspectives on the purpose of the church and its ministry:

- Christian unity
- dialogue with other world religions
- group bias based on race, ethnicity, class or gender

The ecumenical movement came into its own at a time in the twentieth century when Roman Catholic, Protestant, and Orthodox leaders barely knew each other and there was very little basis for trust. It is important, in the 1980s, to remember that barriers, which were once seen as insurmountable, have begun to be broken down and the last quarter century has seen enormous strides toward Christian unity. While the scope of this study does not include the development of ecumenism in this century nor does it pose solutions to the problems remaining in dialogues for Christian unity, it assumes that barriers to ecumenism still remain in theological education.

In many seminaries in North America, a student can move through the entire curriculum and never meet a student of a different denomination. In many more seminaries, such meetings are at best superficial. In some consortia, the possibility of cross-registration is held up as a sign of an ecumenical spirit, but the small percentages of students taking advantage of such opportunities--for the very understandable reasons of limits in time, distance, and the other demands of seminary life--remain as an obstacle to be overcome.

At the same time, the barriers between Protestants and Catholics are not the only ones which exist among Christians today. While the gulf between these two groups has been diminished in the last quarter century, the gulf between liberal and conservative in all branches of Christianity has grown significantly. Cooperative ventures in the future must continue to address Christian unity.

There was also great difficulty in those places where attempts were made to broaden ecumenism to include dialogue among other world religions. While there is consensus that Christian unity is an ideal, however remote, there are conflicting opinions if dialogue with other traditions ought to be included in the theological education enterprise. Buddhist, Muslim, and other traditions are treated as if they were a tiny and curious minority. However, a growing number of North Americans espouse affiliation with these traditions. Moreover, the majority of the world population embraces these religious expressions and technological advances move us toward the global village and bring us into contact with each other.

Christian do view dialogue with the Jewish tradition as a special case and there is more likelihood for agreement among Christian theological educators that dialogue must take place with Jewish scholars, educators, and communities. Yet dialogue among Christians and Jews participates only at the most extreme margins of cooperative ventures. Therefore the study team recommends that cooperative ventures in the future take up the challenge of dialogue among the world religions.

Theological education is characterized by some as a white, male, middle class/upper-middle class enterprise. Certainly the majority of those interviewed for this study fit this description. But the church today is much more diverse. A variety of voices, including people of color, ethnic minorities, and women, are demanding that they not only receive the services of the church, but that the church listen to their voices in the formulation of its policy and its theologies. Some seminaries are attempting to listen and respond. For example, one seminary requires all graduates to be bilingual. But instances of attention to multicultural environments were far too isolated. In the majority of seminaries, the issues of race, class and culture are handled here or there in a social ethics class or in marginal exposure to an institute on Black culture. These issues must be moved to the center of the theological curriculum before schools will be providing a truly meaningful preparation for the demands of ministry in the future.

Perhaps most difficult of all, however, is the issue of gender. The fact that, in many Protestant seminaries, the majority of the student body is now women, while Catholic theological education is struggling with various ways to incorporate the ministry of women within its enterprise, indicates that this issue deserves far more attention than it has received to date. While feminist concerns have been articulated with growing militance and coherence in the past decade, a development undreamed of twenty years ago, these concerns have yet to be incorporated into the heart of the enterprise of theological education. Most consortia have some sort of women's center. A few include more developed institutions for the study of feminist concerns. But none have shown the necessary openness to the insights of feminism as a reforming movement for the whole theological curriculum and for the practice of ministry.

As theological education moves toward the twenty-first century, North American Christians are confronted with a pluralism in their cultures and a technology which links them far more intimately with peoples and countries who once appeared remote. These cultural and technological shifts create issues of communication and bias which affect how Christian perceive their mission and ministry and how they live out their commitments. Theological education is confronted with its tasks to assist Christians in understanding the church's purpose and to develop tools to achieve ministerial excellence. Its tasks can not be done adequately without a commitment to Christian unity, dialogue with other world religions and overcoming group bias.

C. Summary

Chapter I of this report introduced an investigation of cooperation in theological education and Chapter II offered a historical review of the evolution of that cooperation. This review included a survey of several reports which influenced the evolution of theological cooperation.

Chapter III offered the results of a survey on cooperative ventures in theological education and findings from visits to selected sites. These data yielded several factors which are relevant to successful cooperation: leadership, identity, prestige, ecumenism, the focus of attention on programs other than the M. Div. degree, logistical realities and financial resources. The report stressed several other factors for consideration such as historical memory, cooperation which is taken for granted, and changing demographic patterns.

Finally, Chapter IV extrapolated from the findings to discuss the future of theological cooperation. Those who would support cooperative ventures in the 1990s must avoid a dual problem. On the one hand, there is the problem of seeming to impose a single model of cooperation on all seminaries, a move which would be properly resisted by the majority of theological schools today. On the other hand, there is the problem of failing to offer any standards of quality by which cooperative ventures might be measured. This study offers two recommendations to meet this challenge: first, ways to broaden the concept of cooperation, especially in regard to the way cooperative ventures are configured; second, standards for evaluating the purpose of cooperation based on three factors: 1) current understandings of the ministry of the church and the reality of the multiplicity of ministries and the variety of people engaged in those ministries, 2) a re-definition of excellence, and 3) responsiveness to emerging challenges to the ministerial enterprise.

Notes for Chapter IV

1. For further discussion of these models, see Karl E. Weick, "Educational Organizations as Loosely Coupled Systems", *Administrative Science Quarterly* 21, no 1 (March 1976): 1-18 and Karl E. Weick, "Management of Organizational Change among Loosely Coupled Elements" in *Change in Organizations*, edited by Paul Goodman and Associates. San Francisco: Jossey-Bass, 1984.

2. Publication forthcoming.

Appendix I
Sample of Questionnaires

QUESTIONNAIRE FOR BOARD CHAIRPERSON

NAME:_____   DATE:_____

TITLE:_____   YEARS AT INSTITUTION:_____

INSTITUTION:_____   YEARS IN PRESENT POSITION:__

This questionnaire is part of a study about cooperation among
seminaries and in theological education. The purpose of the study
is to assess experience with cooperative activities during the
past two decades, inventory the most significant ventures, and
explore prospects for the future. All ATS accredited, candidate
and associate schools are being sent this survey. In addition,
clusters and consortia listed in the ATS Directory are being
invited to participate.

Cooperation in theological education can take many forms. During
the past twenty years seminaries and schools of theology have
merged programs and entire institutions, combined faculties and
libraries, sponsored lecture series, conferences, and permanent
institutes, and created new programs among themselves or in
cooperation with other institutions, particularly colleges,
universities and church related agencies. In addition,
students, faculty, administrators, trustees and church related
sponsoring bodies have initiated a host of less formal, sometimes
ad hoc, sometimes ongoing ventures with their colleagues in and
outside other schools.

In this survey we have sought a balance between providing some
defined categories of cooperative activity and inviting the
respondents to define and describe their own experiences with
cooperative activity in theological education beyond the
boundaries of their own institution.

Space is provided for your answers. Please attach additional
sheets if necessary. Your participation in the survey is very
much appreciated.

Please return to the Cheswick Center by November 20, 1984.

PART I

This section of the questionnaire asks you to describe the types of cooperation of which your institution has been a part. Listed below are seven different types of cooperation. Please indicate which of the arrangements apply to your school. One or several may apply. If you find that a cooperative arrangement of your school is not accurately defined below, please use Question 8 to identify it.

1. Multipurpose Consortium or Cluster

   Has your institution been involved in a multipurpose consortium or cluster which resulted in several types of ongoing joint activities such as academic cooperation, cross registration, shared services or shared facilities? Yes__ No__ Don't know___

   If yes, please describe the arrangement:

   What other institutions participate(d)?

   Time period: From_____ To_____

2. Single Purpose Consortium or Cluster

   Has your institution ever participated in a single purpose consortium or cluster that resulted primarily in one or two ongoing shared activities? Yes__ No__ Don't know__

   If yes, please describe the arrangement:

   What other institutions participate(d)?

   Time period: From_____ To_____

3. Informal cooperation

Has your institution ever participated in informal cooperative ventures linking departments, faculty members, student organizations or administrative staff on an ad hoc basis?
Yes___ No___ Don't know___

If yes, please describe the arrangement:

What other institutions participate(d)?

Time period: From_____ To_____

4. Corporate Rearrangement

Has your institution ever been involved in a corporate rearrangement in which the governing structure of the merger institutions has been permanently changed (Merger in the typical case)? Yes___ No___ Don't know___

If yes, please describe the arrangement:

What other institutions participate(d)?

Time period: From_____ To_____

5. Joint Research Center

Has your institution ever participated in a joint research or instructional center with other institutions? Yes___ No___ Don't know___

If yes, please describe the arrangement:

What other institutions participate(d)?

Time period: From_____ To_____

6. Academic Institutions of Same Denomination

   Has your institution ever participated in a cooperative venture with other seminaries or academic institutions of the same denomination or religion? Yes__ No__ Don't know__

   If yes, please describe the arrangement:

   What other institutions participate(d)?

   Time period: From_____ To_____

7. Nonacademic Institutions

   Has your institution ever participated in a cooperative venture with nonacademic institutions such as churches, denominational entities, or community organizations? Yes__ No__ Don't know__

   If yes, please describe the arrangement:

   What other institutions participate(d)?

   Time period: From_____ To_____

8. Other Cooperation

   Is there a cooperative venture in which your institution has participated that is not listed in Questions 1-7? Yes__ No__ If there are more than one, please fill in Section b as well.

   a. Please describe the arrangement:

      What other institutions participate (d)?

      Time period: From_____ To_____

   b. Please describe the arrangement:

      What other institutions participate(d)?

      Time period: From_____ To_____

87

PART II

This section of the questionnaire addresses the board's role and attitude concerning cooperative ventures among seminaries and schools of theology.

1. Level of Information

How well informed is the Board regarding cooperative activities of its institution?

___Fully informed

___Adequately informed

___Limited information

___Almost no information

2. Reports on Cooperation

How regularly at Board meetings do you receive reports about the cooperative activities of your institution?

___Every meeting

___Frequently at meetings

___Occasionally at meetings

___Not at all

3. Board Participation on Cooperation

To what extend does the Board participate in decisions about cooperative efforts that the school might undertake? Check as many of the following as apply.

___All new activities are approved by the Board

___On the average we vote on___cooperative activities per year

___Continuing activities are reviewed and approved annually or periodically

___Discontinuation of activities is approved by the Board

___The Board is not involved with decisions concerning cooperation.

___Other

4. Joint Board Activities

Does your Board share authority or responsibility for a cooperative venture with another board? Yes___ No___

If yes, please describe the arrangement:

What other institution(s) and Board(s) participate?

Is there a clear understanding of the roles and authority between the Board(s) responsible for the governance of the cooperative ventures? Yes___ No___ Please explain:

Do one or more members of a Board serve on the other Board(s)? Yes___ No___ Please explain:

5. Cooperation and Board Decisions

Do any of the school's commitments to cooperative ventures influence the Board's decisions?

About the budget? Yes___ No___ Please explain:

About long range planning? Yes___ No___ Please explain:

About fund raising? Yes___ No___ Please explain:

6. Levels of Support

What level of support do the following people affiliated with your school give to cooperative ventures?

	NA	Strongly support	Support	Indifferent	Oppose	Strongly Oppose
Denomination	—	—	—	—	—	—
Governing Board	—	—	—	—	—	—
Religious order	—	—	—	—	—	—
Bishop (Religious Superior)	—	—	—	—	—	—
Faculty	—	—	—	—	—	—
Students	—	—	—	—	—	—
Yourself	—	—	—	—	—	—

89

7. Benefits of Cooperation

In your judgment, have cooperative ventures proved to be beneficial to your institution? Yes__ No__

If so, please check up to four major benefits your institution derives by cooperating.

___a. Furthers ecumenical movement institutionally

___b. Improves student and faculty recruiting

___c. Expands opportunities for study, research and association

___d. Increase opportunities for grants from denominations or foundations

___e. Expands educational opportunities in new fields at minimum cost

___f. Expands field placement opportunities at minimum cost

___g. Provides educational programs and services in geographic areas otherwise inadequately served

___h. Saves money by pooling resources

___i. Expands library resources

___j. Upgrades skill level of staff by sharing resources and information

___k. Other (Please specify)

If not, why have cooperative ventures not been beneficial to your institution?

8. New Ventures

   Does your Board encourage the institution's chief executive to initiate and support cooperative ventures with other institutions? Yes___ No___

   Are new cooperative ventures being explored at this time? Yes___ No___

   If yes, please explain:

Other comments are most appreciated.

Thank you for your help and cooperation.

QUESTIONNAIRE FOR CHIEF EXECUTIVE OFFICER (PRESIDENT)
(Part I is the same as BOARD CHAIRPERSON.)
PART II

If your institution or its members have never participated in a cooperative venture, please go to PART III. PART III asks you to evaluate your cooperative ventures and to explain factors which affect your participation.

1. Most Significant Ventures

From the cooperative ventures that you checked or described in PART I, list up to two that are most significant for your institution.

Venture I   Venture II

_____   _____

2. Activities (Venture I)

For the venture you have listed as Venture I above, please check which of the activities listed below have been included. Then indicate:

Degree of success: Future options:

4-highly successful   4-probably will be expanded
3-successful   3-probably will continue as is
2-partially successful   2-probably will be reduced
1-not successful   1-probably will be discontinued

Example: The Consortium has been identified as the most significant cooperative venture (Venture I) for Seminary A. As part the consortium, library facilities are shared. If the respondent thinks the shared library program has been successful and probably will continue as is, (s)he would fill in the grid as follows:

	Yes	No	Degree of success	Future options
LIBRARY COOPERATION	X		4 ③ 2 1	4 ③ 2 1

Question 2 continued on next page.

2. Activities (Venture I), Continued

Degree of success	Future options
4-highly successful	4-probably will be expanded
3-successful	3-probably will continue as is
2-partially successful	2-probably will be reduced
1-not successful	1-probably will be discontinued

	YES	NO	DEGREE OF SUCCESS	FUTURE OPTIONS
a. SHARED ADMINISTRATION	___	___	4 3 2 1	4 3 2 1
b. PROFESSIONAL DEVELOPMENT FOR ADMINISTRATION	___	___	4 3 2 1	4 3 2 1
c. MUTUAL PUBLIC RELATIONS	___	___	4 3 2 1	4 3 2 1
d. INSTITUTIONAL PLANNING	___	___	4 3 2 1	4 3 2 1
e. MUTUAL FUND RAISING	___	___	4 3 2 1	4 3 2 1
f. JOINT MEETINGS OF THE GOVERNING BOARDS	___	___	4 3 2 1	4 3 2 1
g. CROSS REGISTRATION	___	___	4 3 2 1	4 3 2 1
h. SHARED FACILITIES	___	___	4 3 2 1	4 3 2 1
i. LIBRARY COOPERATION	___	___	4 3 2 1	4 3 2 1
j. STUDENT RECRUITMENT	___	___	4 3 2 1	4 3 2 1
k. ECUMENICAL WORSHIP	___	___	4 3 2 1	4 3 2 1
l. FACULTY HIRING	___	___	4 3 2 1	4 3 2 1
m. FACULTY EXCHANGE	___	___	4 3 2 1	4 3 2 1
n. PROFESSIONAL DEVELOPMENT FOR FACULTY	___	___	4 3 2 1	4 3 2 1
o. CURRICULUM DEVELOPMENT	___	___	4 3 2 1	4 3 2 1
p. FIELD EDUCATION	___	___	4 3 2 1	4 3 2 1
q. DEGREE PROGRAMS	___	___	4 3 2 1	4 3 2 1
r. NONDEGREE PROGRAMS	___	___	4 3 2 1	4 3 2 1
s. SPECIAL EVENTS	___	___	4 3 2 1	4 3 2 1
t. OTHER (PLEASE SPECIFY)	___	___	4 3 2 1	4 3 2 1

3. Activities (Venture II)

For the venture you have listed as Venture II above, please check which of the activities below have been included. Then indicate the degree of success and future options.

Degree of success

4-highly successful
3-successful
2-partially successful
1-not successful

Future options

4-probably will be expanded
3-probably will continue as is
2-probably will be reduced
1-probably will be discontinued

	YES	NO	DEGREE OF SUCCESS				FUTURE OPTIONS			
a. SHARED ADMINISTRATION	___	___	4	3	2	1	4	3	2	1
b. PROFESSIONAL DEVELOPMENT FOR ADMINISTRATION	___	___	4	3	2	1	4	3	2	1
c. MUTUAL PUBLIC RELATIONS	___	___	4	3	2	1	4	3	2	1
d. INSTITUTIONAL PLANNING	___	___	4	3	2	1	4	3	2	1
e. MUTUAL FUND RAISING	___	___	4	3	2	1	4	3	2	1
f. JOINT MEETINGS OF THE GOVERNING BOARDS	___	___	4	3	2	1	4	3	2	1
g. CROSS REGISTRATION	___	___	4	3	2	1	4	3	2	1
h. SHARED FACILITIES	___	___	4	3	2	1	4	3	2	1
i. LIBRARY COOPERATION	___	___	4	3	2	1	4	3	2	1
j. STUDENT RECRUITMENT	___	___	4	3	2	1	4	3	2	1
k. ECUMENICAL WORSHIP	___	___	4	3	2	1	4	3	2	1
l. FACULTY HIRING	___	___	4	3	2	1	4	3	2	1
m. FACULTY EXCHANGE	___	___	4	3	2	1	4	3	2	1
n. PROFESSIONAL DEVELOPMENT FOR FACULTY	___	___	4	3	2	1	4	3	2	1
o. CURRICULUM DEVELOPMENT	___	___	4	3	2	1	4	3	2	1
p. FIELD EDUCATION	___	___	4	3	2	1	4	3	2	1
q. DEGREE PROGRAMS	___	___	4	3	2	1	4	3	2	1
r. NONDEGREE PROGRAMS	___	___	4	3	2	1	4	3	2	1
s. SPECIAL EVENTS	___	___	4	3	2	1	4	3	2	1
t. OTHER (PLEASE SPECIFY)	___	___	4	3	2	1	4	3	2	1

4. Motivations

   Check up to four motivations for your institution's
   participation in cooperative ventures.

   ___a. Further ecumenical movement institutionally

   ___b. Improve student and faculty recruiting by expanding
         opportunities for study, research and association

   ___c. Provide a stimulating environment for learning

   ___d. Increase opportunities for grants from denominations or
         foundations

   ___e. Expand educational opportunities in new fields at minimum
         cost

   ___f. Expand educational placement opportunities at minimum
         cost

   ___g. Provide educational programs and services in geographic
         areas otherwise inadequately served

   ___h. Necessary to save money by pooling human and material
         resources

   ___i. Denomination, church or religious sponsor promoting it

   ___j. Expand library resources by sharing collections

   ___k. Upgrade skill level of staff by sharing resources and
         information

   ___l. Other (Please specify)

5. Benefits

   Check up to four major benefits your institution actually
   derives by cooperating. Letters below correspond to the list
   in Question 4.

   ___a.   ___f.   ___k.

   ___b.   ___g.   ___l. (Please
                                                          specify)
   ___c.   ___h.

   ___d.   ___i.

   ___e.   ___j.

6. Factors Discouraging

List up to four factors that discourage or weaken your school's ability to take part in cooperative ventures.

.

.

.

.

7. Levels of Support

What level of support do the following people affiliated with your school give to cooperative ventures?

	NA	Strongly support	Support	Indif-ferent	Oppose	Strongly Oppose
Denomination	—	—	—	—	—	—
Governing Board	—	—	—	—	—	—
Religious order	—	—	—	—	—	—
Bishop (Religious Superior)	—	—	—	—	—	—
Faculty	—	—	—	—	—	—
Students	—	—	—	—	—	—
Yourself	—	—	—	—	—	—

8. Costs

Evaluate the annual cost to your institution for cooperation. Please circle appropriate answer.

	More than	$25,000-	Less than	Don't
a. Money:	$50,000	$50,000	$25,000	know

	More than	250-	Less than	Don't
b. Time:	750 hours	750 hours	250 hours	know

c. What cooperative activity is most expensive for your school?

What does it cost annually?

d. Did you realize any cost savings or revenue through cooperation? Yes__ No__ Please explain.

96

PART III

PART III asks for your opinion on cooperative activities among seminaries in general and factors which may affect your participation.

1. Financial Situation

   Does your school's financial situation affect its ability or desire to participate in cooperative activities? Yes___ No___

   Please explain:

2. New Cooperation

   Are you exploring participation in a new cooperative venture at this time? Yes___ No___

   If yes, please explain.

3. Cooperation Rejected

   Has your institution ever decided against a cooperative venture? Yes___ No___

   If so, what was the proposal and why did you decide against it?

4. Lessons Learned

   What advice would you give to a president considering a cooperative venture with another institution?

5. Lilly Support

a. What level of importance should the Lilly Endowment give to
   supporting cooperative activities among schools of theology
   and seminaries? Please check one.

   ___High priority, we could definitely use their assistance
      now.

   ___Moderate priority, we can probably use their assistance now.

   ___Low priority, we would prefer that they fund_____.

b. How can the Lilly Endowment best support cooperative ventures?
   (e.g., technical assistance, funding, etc.)

c. What kind of cooperative efforts should receive priority?

Thank you for your time and cooperation

QUESTIONNAIRE FOR CHIEF ACADEMIC OFFICER (DEAN)
(Part I is the same as BOARD CHAIRPERSON.)

PART II

If your institution or its members have never participated in a
cooperative venture, please go to PART III. PART II asks you to
evaluate your cooperative ventures and to explain factors which
affect your participation.

1. Most Significant Ventures

   From the cooperative ventures that you checked or described in
   PART I, list up to two that are most significant for your
   institution.

   Venture I   Venture II

   _____   _____

2. Activities (Venture I)

   For the venture you have listed as Venture I above, please
   check which of the activities listed below have been included.
   Then indicate:

   Degree of success: Future options:

   4-highly successful   4-probably will be expanded
   3-successful   3-probably will continue as is
   2-partially successful   2-probably will be reduced
   1-not successful   1-probably will be discontinued

   Example: The Consortium has been identified as the most
   significant cooperative venture (Venture I) for Seminary A. As
   part the consortium, library facilities are shared. If the
   respondent thinks the shared library program has been
   successful and probably will continue as is, (s)he would fill
   in the grid as follows:

	Yes	No	Degree of success	Future options
LIBRARY COOPERATION	X		4 ③ 2 1	4 ③ 2 1

   Question 2 continued on next page.

99

2. Activities (Venture I), Continued

Degree of success

4-highly successful
3-successful
2-partially successful
1-not successful

Future options

4-probably will be expanded
3-probably will continue as is
2-probably will be reduced
1-probably will be discontinued

	YES	NO	DEGREE OF SUCCESS				FUTURE OPTIONS			
a. PROFESSIONAL DEVELOPMENT FOR DEANS	___	___	4	3	2	1	4	3	2	1
b. CROSS REGISTRATION	___	___	4	3	2	1	4	3	2	1
c. LIBRARY COOPERATION	___	___	4	3	2	1	4	3	2	1
d. STUDENT RECRUITMENT	___	___	4	3	2	1	4	3	2	1
e. ECUMENICAL WORSHIP	___	___	4	3	2	1	4	3	2	1
f. FACULTY HIRING	___	___	4	3	2	1	4	3	2	1
g. FACULTY EXCHANGE	___	___	4	3	2	1	4	3	2	1
h. PROFESSIONAL DEVELOPMENT FOR FACULTY	___	___	4	3	2	1	4	3	2	1
i. CURRICULUM DEVELOPMENT	___	___	4	3	2	1	4	3	2	1
j. FIELD EDUCATION	___	___	4	3	2	1	4	3	2	1
k. DEGREE PROGRAMS	___	___	4	3	2	1	4	3	2	1
l. NONDEGREE PROGRAMS	___	___	4	3	2	1	4	3	2	1
m. JOINT PROGRAM ADMINISTRATION	___	___	4	3	2	1	4	3	2	1
n. OTHER (PLEASE SPECIFY)	___	___	4	3	2	1	4	3	2	1

3. Activities (Venture II)

For the venture you have listed as Venture II above, please
check which of the activities below have been included. Then
indicate the degree of success and future options.

Degree of success   Future options

4-highly successful   4-probably will be expanded
3-successful   3-probably will continue as is
2-partially successful   2-probably will be reduced
1-not successful   1-probably will be discontinued

	YES	NO	DEGREE OF SUCCESS				FUTURE OPTIONS			
a. PROFESSIONAL DEVELOPMENT FOR DEANS	___	___	4	3	2	1	4	3	2	1
b. CROSS REGISTRATION	___	___	4	3	2	1	4	3	2	1
c. LIBRARY COOPERATION	___	___	4	3	2	1	4	3	2	1
d. STUDENT RECRUITMENT	___	___	4	3	2	1	4	3	2	1
e. ECUMENICAL WORSHIP	___	___	4	3	2	1	4	3	2	1
f. FACULTY HIRING	___	___	4	3	2	1	4	3	2	1
g. FACULTY EXCHANGE	___	___	4	3	2	1	4	3	2	1
h. PROFESSIONAL DEVELOPMENT FOR FACULTY	___	___	4	3	2	1	4	3	2	1
i. CURRICULUM DEVELOPMENT	___	___	4	3	2	1	4	3	2	1
j. FIELD EDUCATION	___	___	4	3	2	1	4	3	2	1
k. DEGREE PROGRAMS	___	___	4	3	2	1	4	3	2	1
l. NONDEGREE PROGRAMS	___	___	4	3	2	1	4	3	2	1
m. JOINT PROGRAM ADMINISTRATION	___	___	4	3	2	1	4	3	2	1
n. OTHER (PLEASE SPECIFY)	___	___	4	3	2	1	4	3	2	1

4. Motivations

   Check up to four motivations for your institution's
   participation in cooperative ventures.

   ___a. Further ecumenical movement institutionally

   ___b. Improve student and faculty recruiting by expanding
        opportunities for study, research and association

   ___c. Provide a stimulating environment for learning

   ___d. Increase opportunities for grants from denominations or
        foundations

   ___e. Expand educational opportunities in new fields at minimum
        cost

   ___f. Expand field placement opportunities at minimum cost

   ___g. Provide educational programs and services in geographic
        areas otherwise inadequately served

   ___h. Necessary to save money by pooling human and material
        resources

   ___i. Denomination, church or religious sponsor promoting it

   ___j. Expand library resources by sharing collections

   ___k. Upgrade skill level of staff by sharing resources and
        information

   ___l. Other (Please specify)

5. Benefits

   Check up to four major benefits your institution actually
   derives by cooperating. Letters below correspond to the list
   in Question 4.

   ___a.   ___f.   ___k.

   ___b.   ___g.   ___l. (Please
                                                      specify)
   ___c.   ___h.

   ___d.   ___i.

   ___e.   ___j.

6. Factors Discouraging

   List up to four factors that discourage or weaken your school's
   ability to take part in cooperative ventures.

   .

   .

   .

   .

7. Levels of Support

   What level of support do the following people affiliated with
   your school give to cooperative ventures?

	NA	Strongly support	Support	Indif-ferent	Oppose	Strongly Oppose
Denomination	—	—	—	—	—	—
Governing Board	—	—	—	—	—	—
Religious order	—	—	—	—	—	—
Bishop (Religious Superior)	—	—	—	—	—	—
Faculty	—	—	—	—	—	—
Students	—	—	—	—	—	—
Yourself	—	—	—	—	—	—

PART III

PART III asks for your opinion on cooperative activities among seminaries in general and factors which may affect your participation.

1. Financial Situation

   Does your school's financial situation affect its ability or desire to participate in cooperative activities?

   Yes   No
   Please explain:

2. New Cooperation

   Are you exploring participation in a new cooperative venture at this time?

   Yes   No

   If yes, please explain.

3. Students and Cooperation

   How will the changing composition and numbers of students affect your institution's ability or desire to participate in cooperative ventures?

4. Employment and Cooperation

   How will changing possibilities for employment for graduates affect your institution's ability or desire to participate in cooperative ventures?

5. Lilly Support

a. What level of importance should the Lilly Endowment give to
   supporting cooperative activities among schools of theology
   and seminaries? Please check one.

   ___High priority, we could definitely use their assistance
       right now.

   ___Moderate priority, we can probably use their assistance now

   ___Low priority, we would prefer that they fund_____

b. How can the Lilly Endowment best support cooperative ventures?
   (e.g., technical assistance, funding, etc.)

c. What kind of cooperative efforts should receive priority?

Thank you for your time and cooperation.

QUESTIONNAIRE FOR FACULTY
(Part I is the same as BOARD CHAIRPERSON.)

PART II

PART II asks you to evaluate your institution's cooperative ventures and to explain factors which affect its success or inadequacies.

1. Most Significant Ventures

   From the cooperative ventures that you checked or described in PART I, list up to two that are most significant for your institution.

   Venture I   Venture II

   _____   _____

2. Activities (Venture I)

   For the venture you have listed as Venture I above, please check which of the activities listed below have been included. Then indicate:

   Degree of success: Future options:

   4-highly successful   4-probably will be expanded
   3-successful   3-probably will continue as is
   2-partially successful   2-probably will be reduced
   1-not successful   1-probably will be discontinued

   Example: The Consortium has been identified as the most significant cooperative venture (Venture I) for Seminary A. As part the consortium, library facilities are shared. If the respondent thinks the shared library program has been successful and probably will continue as is, (s)he would fill in the grid as follows:

	Yes	No	Degree of success				Future options			
LIBRARY COOPERATION	X		4	3	2	1	4	3	2	1

Question 2 continued on next page.

2. Activities (Venture I), Continued

Degree of success	Future options
4-highly successful	4-probably will be expanded
3-successful	3-probably will continue as is
2-partially successful	2-probably will be reduced
1-not successful	1-probably will be discontinued

	YES	NO	DEGREE OF SUCCESS				FUTURE OPTIONS			
a. CROSS REGISTRATION	___	___	4	3	2	1	4	3	2	1
b. SHARED FACILITIES	___	___	4	3	2	1	4	3	2	1
c. LIBRARY COOPERATION	___	___	4	3	2	1	4	3	2	1
d. ECUMENICAL WORSHIP	___	___	4	3	2	1	4	3	2	1
e. JOINT FACULTY APPOINTMENTS	___	___	4	3	2	1	4	3	2	1
f. FACULTY EXCHANGE	___	___	4	3	2	1	4	3	2	1
g. PROFESSIONAL DEVELOPMENT FOR FACULTY	___	___	4	3	2	1	4	3	2	1
h. CURRICULUM DEVELOPMENT	___	___	4	3	2	1	4	3	2	1
i. FACULTY ADVISING STUDENTS FROM OTHER ORGANIZATIONS	___	___	4	3	2	1	4	3	2	1
j. FIELD EDUCATION	___	___	4	3	2	1	4	3	2	1
k. SHARED DEGREE PROGRAM(S)	___	___	4	3	2	1	4	3	2	1
l. SHARED NONDEGREE PROGRAM(S)	___	___	4	3	2	1	4	3	2	1
m. PARTICIPATION IN COMMITTEE WORK OF COOPERATIVE VENTURE	___	___	4	3	2	1	4	3	2	1
n. JOINT RESEARCH	___	___	4	3	2	1	4	3	2	1
o. OTHER (PLEASE SPECIFY)	___	___	4	3	2	1	4	3	2	1

3. Activities (Venture II)

For the venture you have listed as Venture II above, please
check which of the activities below have been included. Then
indicate the degree of success and future options.

Degree of success   Future options

4-highly successful   4-probably will be expanded
3-successful   3-probably will continue as is
2-partially successful   2-probably will be reduced
1-not successful   1-probably will be discontinued

		YES	NO	DEGREE OF SUCCESS				FUTURE OPTIONS			
a.	CROSS REGISTRATION	___	___	4	3	2	1	4	3	2	1
b.	SHARED FACILITIES	___	___	4	3	2	1	4	3	2	1
c.	LIBRARY COOPERATION	___	___	4	3	2	1	4	3	2	1
d.	ECUMENICAL WORSHIP	___	___	4	3	2	1	4	3	2	1
e.	JOINT FACULTY APPOINTMENTS	___	___	4	3	2	1	4	3	2	1
f.	FACULTY EXCHANGE	___	___	4	3	2	1	4	3	2	1
g.	PROFESSIONAL DEVELOPMENT FOR FACULTY	___	___	4	3	2	1	4	3	2	1
h.	CURRICULUM DEVELOPMENT	___	___	4	3	2	1	4	3	2	1
i.	FACULTY ADVISING STUDENTS FROM OTHER ORGANIZATIONS	___	___	4	3	2	1	4	3	2	1
j.	FIELD EDUCATION	___	___	4	3	2	1	4	3	2	1
k.	SHARED DEGREE PROGRAM(S)	___	___	4	3	2	1	4	3	2	1
l.	SHARED NONDEGREE PROGRAM(S)	___	___	4	3	2	1	4	3	2	1
m.	PARTICIPATION IN COMMITTEE WORK OF COOPERATIVE VENTURE	___	___	4	3	2	1	4	3	2	1
n.	JOINT RESEARCH	___	___	4	3	2	1	4	3	2	1
o.	OTHER (PLEASE SPECIFY)	___	___	4	3	2	1	4	3	2	1

4. Benefits

Check up to four major benefits to faculty of cooperation at their institution.

____a. Further ecumenical movement

____b. Improve student and faculty recruitment

____c. Increase opportunities for study, research and association

____d. Increase opportunities for grants from denominations or foundations

____e. Expand field placement opportunities

____f. Provide educational programs and services in geographic areas otherwise inadequately served

____g. Save money by pooling resources

____h. Expand library resources

____i. Upgrade skill level of staff by sharing resources and information

____j. Increase faculty enrichment by providing stimulating environment for learning

____k. Administration of courses more efficient

____l. Other (Please specify)

5. Difficulties

What are the difficulties for faculty of participating in cooperative ventures?

6. End of Cooperation

What would be the consequences to the faculty if cooperation ceased?

7. Changes in Cooperation

How has cooperation changed during your time at the institution?

8. Levels of Support

What level of support do the following people affiliated with your school give to cooperative ventures?

	NA	Strongly support	Support	Indif- ferent	Oppose	Strongly Oppose
Denomination	—	—	—	—	—	—
Governing Board	—	—	—	—	—	—
Religious order	—	—	—	—	—	—
Bishop (Religious Superior)	—	—	—	—	—	—
Faculty	—	—	—	—	—	—
Students	—	—	—	—	—	—
Yourself	—	—	—	—	—	—

9. Lilly Support

   a. What level of importance should the Lilly Endowment give to
      supporting cooperative activities among schools of theology
      and seminaries: Please check one.

      ___High priority, we could definitely use their assistance
         now.

      ___Moderate priority, we can probably use their assistance
         now.

      ___Low priority, we would prefer that they fund_____.

   b. How can the Lilly Endowment best support cooperative
      ventures? (e.g., technical assistance, funding, etc.)

   c. What kind of cooperative efforts should receive priority?

Thank you for your time and cooperation.

QUESTIONNAIRE FOR LIBRARIAN
(Part I is the same as BOARD CHAIRPERSON.)

PART II

If your institution or its members have participated in a
cooperative venture, please complete PART II. PART II asks you to
evaluate your cooperative ventures and to explain factors which
affect your participation.

1. Most Significant Ventures

   From the cooperative ventures that you checked or described in
   PART I, list up to two that are most significant for your
   institution.

   Venture I   Venture II

   _____   _____

2. Activities (Venture I)

   For the venture you have listed as Venture I above, please
   check which of the activities listed below have been included.
   Then indicate:

   Degree of success: Future options:

   4-highly successful   4-probably will be expanded
   3-successful   3-probably will continue as is
   2-partially successful   2-probably will be reduced
   1-not successful   1-probably will be discontinued

   Example: The Consortium has been identified as the most
   significant cooperative venture (Venture I) for Seminary A. As
   part the consortium, computer services are shared. If the
   respondent thinks the shared computer services program has
   been successful and probably will continue as is, (s)he would
   fill in the grid as follows:

	Yes	No	Degree of success				Future options			
SHARED COMPUTER SERVICES	x		4	3	2	1	4	3	2	1

Question 2 continued on next page.

112

2. Activities (Venture I), Continued

Degree of success   Future options

    4-highly successful   4-probably will be expanded
    3-successful   3-probably will continue as is
    2-partially successful   2-probably will be reduced
    1-not successful   1-probably will be discontinued

	YES	NO	DEGREE OF SUCCESS				FUTURE OPTIONS			
a. JOINT LIBRARY FACILITY UNDER ONE ADMINISTRATION	___	___	4	3	2	1	4	3	2	1
b. PROFESSIONAL DEVELOPMENT FOR LIBRARIANS	___	___	4	3	2	1	4	3	2	1
c. STAFF DEVELOPMENT	___	___	4	3	2	1	4	3	2	1
d. BORROWING PRIVILEGES AT OTHER INSTITUTIONS	___	___	4	3	2	1	4	3	2	1
e. MESSENGER SERVICES	___	___	4	3	2	1	4	3	2	1
f. INTERLIBRARY LOANS	___	___	4	3	2	1	4	3	2	1
g. ACQUISITIONN PLANNING	___	___	4	3	2	1	4	3	2	1
h. UNION LISTS	___	___	4	3	2	1	4	3	2	1
i. POLICY PLANNING	___	___	4	3	2	1	4	3	2	1
j. DEVELOPMENT OF JOINT GRANTS	___	___	4	3	2	1	4	3	2	1
k. SHARED COMPUTER SERVICES	___	___	4	3	2	1	4	3	2	1
l. SPECIAL EVENTS (PLEASE SPECIFY)	___	___	4	3	2	1	4	3	2	1
m. OTHER (PLEASE SPECIFY)	___	___	4	3	2	1	4	3	2	1

3. Activities (Venture II)

For the venture you have listed as Venture II above, please
check which of the activities below have been included. Then
indicate the degree of success and future options.

Degree of success   Future options

4-highly successful   4-probably will be expanded
3-successful   3-probably will continue as is
2-partially successful   2-probably will be reduced
1-not successful   1-probably will be discontinued

	YES	NO	DEGREE OF SUCCESS				FUTURE OPTIONS			
a. JOINT LIBRARY FACILITY UNDER ONE ADMINISTRATION	___	___	4	3	2	1	4	3	2	1
b. PROFESSIONAL DEVELOPMENT FOR LIBRARIANS	___	___	4	3	2	1	4	3	2	1
c. STAFF DEVELOPMENT	___	___	4	3	2	1	4	3	2	1
d. BORROWING PRIVILEGES AT OTHER INSTITUTIONS	___	___	4	3	2	1	4	3	2	1
e. MESSENGER SERVICES	___	___	4	3	2	1	4	3	2	1
f. INTERLIBRARY LOANS	___	___	4	3	2	1	4	3	2	1
g. ACQUISITION PLANNING	___	___	4	3	2	1	4	3	2	1
h. UNION LISTS	___	___	4	3	2	1	4	3	2	1
i. POLICY PLANNING	___	___	4	3	2	1	4	3	2	1
j. DEVELOPMENT OF JOINT GRANTS	___	___	4	3	2	1	4	3	2	1
k. SHARED COMPUTER SERVICES	___	___	4	3	2	1	4	3	2	1
l. SPECIAL EVENTS (PLEASE SPECIFY)	___	___	4	3	2	1	4	3	2	1
m. OTHER (PLEASE SPECIFY)	___	___	4	3	2	1	4	3	2	1

4. Benefits

Check up to four major benefits your institution actually derives by cooperating.

___a. Further ecumenical movement institutionally

___b. Improve student and faculty recruiting by expanding opportunities for study, research and association

___c. Provide a stimulating environment for learning

___d. Increase opportunities for grants from denominations or foundations

___e. Expand educational opportunities in new fields at minimum cost

___f. Expand educational placement opportunities at minimum cost

___g. Provide educational programs and services in geographic areas otherwise inadequately served

___h. Necessary to save money by pooling human material resources

___i. Denomination, church or religious sponsor promoting it

___j. Expand library resources by sharing collections

___k. Upgrade skill level of staff by sharing resources and information

___l. Other (Please specify)

5. Disadvantages

List up to four major disadvantages to your institution of cooperating

.

.

.

.

6. Personal Participation

Please describe your personal participation and extent of involvement in the cooperative venture(s). Also indicate how much of your time it takes

7. Changes in Cooperation

How has cooperation changed during your employment as librarian? Please explain if the change has been a loss or gain to your library.

8. End of Cooperation

If cooperation cease, how would your library be different? Would there be other ways to obtain lost services?

9. Future Cooperation

What areas would you target for future cooperation?

Thank you for your time and cooperation. We would also appreciate receiving any other documents, reports or guidelines on interlibrary cooperation which may be helpful in our study.

PART II

If your institution or its members have participated in a
cooperative venture, please complete PART II. PART II asks you to
evaluate your cooperative ventures and to explain factors which
affect your participation.

1. Most Significant Ventures

   From the cooperative ventures that you checked or described in
   PART I, list up to two that are most significant for you as
   Registrar.

   Venture I   Venture II

   _____   _____

2. Activities (Venture I)

   For the venture you have listed as Venture I above, please
   check which of the activities listed below have been included.
   Then indicate:

   Degree of success: Future options:

   4-highly successful   4-probably will be expanded
   3-successful   3-probably will continue as is
   2-partially successful   2-probably will be reduced
   1-not successful   1-probably will be discontinued

   Example: The Consortium has been identified as the most
   significant cooperative venture (Venture I) for Seminary A. As
   part the consortium, computer services are shared. If the
   respondent thinks the shared computer services program has
   been successful and probably will continue as is, (s)he would
   fill in the grid as follows:

                         Yes No   Degree of success   Future options

   SHARED COMPUTER
   SERVICES   x   4   3   2   1   4   3   2   1

   Question 2 continued on next page.

2. Activities (Venture I), Continued

Degree of success	Future options
4-highly successful	4-probably will be expanded
3-successful	3-probably will continue as is
2-partially successful	2-probably will be reduced
1-not successful	1-probably will be discontinued

	YES	NO	DEGREE OF SUCCESS	FUTURE OPTIC
a. CROSS REGISTRATION	___	___	4 3 2 1	4 3 2
b. EXCHANGE OF TRANSCRIPTS	___	___	4 3 2 1	4 3 2
c. PROFESSIONAL DEVELOPMENT OF REGISTRARS	___	___	4 3 2 1	4 3 2
d. SHARED COMPUTER SERVICES	___	___	4 3 2 1	4 3 2
e. JOINT RECORD KEEPING	___	___	4 3 2 1	4 3 2
f. JOINT REGISTRAR	___	___	4 3 2 1	4 3 2
g. OTHER (PLEASE SPECIFY)	___	___	4 3 2 1	4 3 2

3. <u>Activities</u> <u>(Venture II)</u>

For the venture you have listed as Venture II above, please
check which of the activities below have been included. Then
indicate the degree of success and future options.

Degree of success   Future options

4-highly successful   4-probably will be expanded
3-successful   3-probably will continue as is
2-partially successful   2-probably will be reduced
1-not successful   1-probably will be discontinued

	<u>YES</u>	<u>NO</u>	<u>DEGREE</u> <u>OF</u> <u>SUCCESS</u>				<u>FUTURE</u> <u>OPTIONS</u>			
a. CROSS REGISTRATION	___	___	4	3	2	1	4	3	2	1
b. EXCHANGE OF TRANSCRIPTS	___	___	4	3	2	1	4	3	2	1
c. PROFESSIONAL DEVELOPMENT OF REGISTRARS	___	___	4	3	2	1	4	3	2	1
d. SHARED COMPUTER SERVICES	___	___	4	3	2	1	4	3	2	1
e. JOINT RECORD KEEPING	___	___	4	3	2	1	4	3	2	1
f. JOINT REGISTRAR	___	___	4	3	2	1	4	3	2	1
g. OTHER (PLEASE SPECIFY)	___	___	4	3	2	1	4	3	2	1

119

4. Benefits

What are benefits of cooperation for you as Registrar?

5. Disadvantages

What are the disadvantages of cooperation for you?

6. Future Cooperation

What areas would you target for future cooperation?

PART III

PART III asks you to supply specific information about enrollment, cross registration and tuition policy at your institution.

1. How many students were enrolled at your institution during the 1983-84 school year?

   Fall semester_____   Spring semester_____

2. Does your institution have cross registration? Yes__ No__

   If yes, please fill in below or attach separately the cross registration figures for the past five years.

   a. Number of students from your institution registered at other schools

Fall 1979	Spring 1980	F 1980	S 1981	F 1981	S 1982	F 1982	S 1983	F 1983	S 1984
___	___	___	___	___	___	___	___	___	___

   b. Number of students from other institutions registered at your school?

Fall 1979	Spring 1980	1980	1981	1981	1982	1982	1983	1983	1984
___	___	___	___	___	___	___	___	___	___

3. Cross Registration Policy

   a. Does your institution require students in various degree
      programs to cross register? Yes___ No___

      If yes, please explain:

   b. Does your institution limit the number of courses students
      may take for credit at other institutions? Yes___ No___

      If yes, please explain:

   c. What other policies does your institution have regarding
      cross registration? If there is a written copy, we would
      appreciate receiving a copy.

4. Tuition for Cross Registration

   If your institution has cross registration, check the answer
   below which describes how tuition for cross registration is
   paid.

   ___Paid by student to home institution

   ___Paid by student to host institution

   ___Paid by home to host institution

   ___No additional fee

   ___Other (Please specify)

Thank you for your time and cooperation.

QUESTIONNAIRE FOR STUDENT LEADER
(Part I is the same as BOARD CHAIRPERSON.)

PART II

PART II asks you to evaluate your institution's cooperative ventures and to explain factors which affect its success or inadequacies.

1. Most Significant Ventures

   From the cooperative ventures that you checked or described in PART I, list up to two that are most significant for your institution.

   Venture I   Venture II

   _____   _____

2. Activities (Venture I)

   For the venture you have listed as Venture I above, please check which of the activities listed below have been included. Then indicate:

   Degree of success: Future options:

   4-highly successful   4-probably will be expanded
   3-successful   3-probably will continue as is
   2-partially successful   2-probably will be reduced
   1-not successful   1-probably will be discontinued

   Example: The Consortium has been identified as the most significant cooperative venture (Venture I) for Seminary A. As part the consortium, library facilities are shared. If the respondent thinks the shared library program has been successful and probably will continue as is, (s)he would fill in the grid as follows:

	Yes	No	Degree of success	Future options
LIBRARY COOPERATION	X		4 (3) 2 1	4 (3) 2 1

   Question 2 continued on next page.

2. Activities (Venture I), Continued

Degree of success

4-highly successful
3-successful
2-partially successful
1-not successful

Future options

4-probably will be expanded
3-probably will continue as is
2-probably will be reduced
1-probably will be discontinued

	YES	NO	DEGREE OF SUCCESS				FUTURE OPTIONS			
a. CROSS REGISTRATION	___	___	4	3	2	1	4	3	2	1
b. FACULTY FROM OTHER INSTITUTIONS TEACHING AT YOUR SCHOOL	___	___	4	3	2	1	4	3	2	1
c. SHARED CORE COURSES	___	___	4	3	2	1	4	3	2	1
d. SHARED DEGREE PROGRAMS	___	___	4	3	2	1	4	3	2	1
e. SHARED NONDEGREE PROGRAMS	___	___	4	3	2	1	4	3	2	1
f. ECUMENICAL WORSHIP	___	___	4	3	2	1	4	3	2	1
g. JOINT STUDENT ORGANIZATIONS	___	___	4	3	2	1	4	3	2	1
h. SHARED FIELD EDUCATION PROGRAMS	___	___	4	3	2	1	4	3	2	1
i. CONTACT WITH FACULTY FROM OTHER INSTITUTIONS OUTSIDE OF CLASS	___	___	4	3	2	1	4	3	2	1
j. OTHER (PLEASE SPECIFY)	___	___	4	3	2	1	4	3	2	1

3. Activities (Venture II)

For the venture you have listed as Venture II above, please
check which of the activities below have been included. Then
indicate the degree of success and future options.

Degree of success   Future options

4-highly successful   4-probably will be expanded
3-successful   3-probably will continue as is
2-partially successful   2-probably will be reduced
1-not successful   1-probably will be discontinued

	YES	NO	DEGREE OF SUCCESS				FUTURE OPTIONS			
a. CROSS REGISTRATION	___	___	4	3	2	1	4	3	2	1
b. FACULTY FROM OTHER INSTITUTIONS TEACHING AT YOUR SCHOOL	___	___	4	3	2	1	4	3	2	1
c. SHARED CORE COURSES	___	___	4	3	2	1	4	3	2	1
d. SHARED DEGREE PROGRAMS	___	___	4	3	2	1	4	3	2	1
e. SHARED NONDEGREE PROGRAMS	___	___	4	3	2	1	4	3	2	1
f. ECUMENICAL WORSHIP	___	___	4	3	2	1	4	3	2	1
g. JOINT STUDENT ORGANIZATIONS	___	___	4	3	2	1	4	3	2	1
h. SHARED FIELD EDUCATION PROGRAMS	___	___	4	3	2	1	4	3	2	1
i. CONTACT WITH FACULTY FROM OTHER INSTITUTIONS OUTSIDE OF CLASS	___	___	4	3	2	1	4	3	2	1
j. OTHER (PLEASE SPECIFY)	___	___	4	3	2	1	4	3	2	1

4. Cooperation and Application to School

Was your institution,s participation in cooperative ventures a consideration for you when applying to the school? Yes__ No__

If yes, which of the following benefits of cooperation did you anticipate? Please check no more than three.

___a. Opportunity to learn about other faith traditions

___b. Sense of unity with other denominations

___c. A stimulating environment for learning

___d. Expanded opportunities for study, research and association

___e. Expanded field placement opportunities

___f. Expanded library resources

___g. Additional educational programs and services in geographic areas otherwise inadequately served

___h. Other (Please specify)

5. Benefits

Check up to three major benefits of cooperation students actually desire. Letters below correspond to the list in Question 4.

___a.   ___e.

___b.   ___f.

___c.   ___g.

___d   ___h.

6. Difficulties

What are the difficulties for students of participating in cooperative ventures?

-
-
-
-

7. Ending Cooperation

What would be the consequences to students if cooperation ceased?

8. Views on Cooperation

Please indicate by a check which of the following statements about cooperative ventures best represents your view, the view of the majority of students and the view of the administration.

	Your view	Students	Administration
a. Cooperative ventures with other seminaries are essential to providing quality education at our school or seminary			
b. While not essential, cooperative ventures make our seminary or school a much better educational vehicle for students and faculty			
c. Cooperative ventures are a small aspect of the educational quality of our school or seminary.			
d. Cooperative ventures undermine the integrity of our institution and confuse its educational purpose.			

9. Foundation Support

  a. What level of importance should an outside funding
     organization give to promoting cooperative activities among
     seminaries and schools of theology?

     ___Very important, we could definitely use funding for this
        now

     ___Somewhat important, we could probably use funding for
        this now

     ___Not important for the near future, we would rather it
        focus on_____

  b. What kind of cooperative efforts should receive priority?

Other comments are most appreciated.

Thank you for your time and cooperation

Appendix II
List of Interviewees

Institutional identifications at the time of the interview

Nikolaos Apostola, Former Student, Holy Cross Greek Orthodox School of Theology, Brookline, MA

Carol Baker, Registrar, Luther Northwestern Theological Seminary, St. Paul, MN

Lance Barker, Director of D.Min. Program, United Theological Seminary, New Brighton, MN

Robert Barr, President, San Francisco Theological Seminary, San Anselmo, CA

Clarence Bass, Faculty, Bethel Theological Seminary, St. Paul. MN

William Baumgaertner, Associate Director, Association of Theological Schools, Vandalia, OH

Allan Beattie, Board, Toronto School of Theology, Toronto, Ontario, Canada

Robert Bellah, Faculty, University of California, Berkeley; Graduate Theological Union, Berkeley, CA

Wilbur K. Benningfield, Dean, Baptist MIssionary Association Theological Seminary, Jackson, TX

Lauri Bethel, Student, American Baptist Seminary of the West, Berkeley, CA

Colin Bircumshaw, Rector-President, Pontifial College Josephinum, Columbus, OH

Claudia Blanchette, S.N.D., Director, Educational and Pastoral Ministry, Emmanuel College, Boston, MA

Michael Blecker, O.S.B., President, Graduate Theological Union, Berkeley, CA

Carol Bohn, Faculty, Boston University School of Theology, Boston, MA

David J. Bowman, S.J., Assistant Director for Ecumenism, Chicago, IL

R. Grant Bracewell, Library Coordinator, Toronto School of Theology, Toronto, Ontario, Canada

Josephine Brandt, Registrar, Lutheran School of Theology in Chicago, Chicago, IL

Ann Brotherton, Director of Field Education, Jesuit School of Theology, Berkeley, CA

Wesley Brown, President, American Baptist Seminary of the West, Berkeley, CA

Philip R. Bryan, Faculty, Baptist Missionary Association Theological Seminary, Jackson, TX

Paddy-Ann Burns, Toronto School of Theology, Toronto School of Theology, Toronto, Ontario, Canada

Thomas Byrne, Director of Formation, Holy Ghost Fathers, Oblate School of Theology, San Antonio, TX

Alkivides Calivas, Dean, Holy Cross Greek Orthodox School of Theology, Brookline, MA

Donald Cameron, Board, Toronto School of Theology, Toronto, Ontario, Canada

Francine Cardman, Faculty, Weston School of Theology, Cambridge, MA

Charles Carter, Executive Vice President, Golden Gate Baptist Theological Seminary, Mill Valley, CA

R. Michael Casto, Commission on Interprofessional Education, Ohio State University, Columbus, OH

William H. Casto, Jr., Assoc. Director of Field Education, Methesco, Delaware, OH

Robert L. Cate, Dean, Golden Gate Baptist Theological Seminary, Mill Valley, CA
Gail Chambers, Research Consultant, Conference of Small Private Colleges, Princeton,
    NJ
Jennifer Corbett, OSF, Student, Catholic Theological Union, Chicago, IL
James Costen, President, Interdenominational Theological Center, Atlanta, GA
Charles Cousar, Columbia Theological Seminary, Decatur, GA
Donald Coxe, Board, Toronto School of Theology, Toronto, Ontario, Canada
Mary Cross, Director, Center for Women and Religion, Graduate Theological Union,
    Berkeley, CA
Vincent de Gregoris, Eastern Baptist Theological Seminary, Philadelphia, PA
Joanne Dewart, Assist. Director for Advanced Degree Studies, Toronto School of
    Theology, Toronto, Ontario, Canada
John C. Diamond, Jr., Faculty, Interdenominational Theological Center, Atlanta, GA
Herminal Diaz, Director of the Hispanic Program,Wartburg Theological Seminary at
    Austin, Austin, TX
John Dillenberger, Founder, Graduate Theological Union, Berkeley, CA
Jerome Dittberner, Faculty, St. Paul Seminary, St. Paul. MN
D. Richard Doherty, Student, Toronto School of Theology, Toronto, Ontario, Canada
Lisa Doucette, Director of Development, Boston Theological Institute, Cambridge,
    MA
Doris Dyke, Faculty, Emmanuel College, Toronto, Ontario, Canada
Eldon Ernst, Faculty, Franciscan School of Theology and Graduate Theological Union,
    Berkeley, CA
Eugene Fairweather, Dean, Trinity College, Toronto, Ontario, Canada
John Farrell, Academic Dean, St. John's Seminary, Brighton, MA
Robert A. Featherstone, Associate Dean of Administration, Bethel Theological
    Seminary, St. Paul, MN
Kula FitzGerald, Pastoral Counselor, Holy Cross Greek Orthodox School of Theology,
    Brookline, MA
Stuart Frayne, Assistant Director for Continuing Education, Toronto School of
    Theology, Toronto, Ontario, Canada
Terence Fretheim, President of the Consortium, Academic Dean, Luther Northwestern
    Theological School, St. Paul. Mn
Charles Froehle, Rector, St. Paul Seminary, St. Paul, MN
Neil Gerdes, Librarian, Chicago Theological Seminary, Chicago, IL
Lorine Getz, Executive Director, Boston Theological Institute, Newton Centre, MA
Victor Gold, Dean, Pacific Lutheran Theological School, Berkeley, CA
Catherine G. Gonzalez, Proefessor of Church History, Columbia Theological School,
    Decatur, GA
Patrick Guidon, President, Oblate School of Theology, San Antonio, TX
Louis H. Guinnemann, Adjunct Professor of Ministerial Studies, United Theological
    Seminary, New Brighton, MN
John Haas, Treasurer and Faculty, Pontifical College Josephinum, Columbus, OH
J. Charles Hay, Principal, Knox College, Toronto, Ontario, Canada
William Hand, Chaplain, Eastern Baptist Theological School, Philadelphia, PA
Joe Harris, Director of Formation, Holy Ghost Fathers, Chicago Cluster, Chicago, IL
Roland Harrison, Principal, Wycliffe College, Toronto, Ontario, Canada

John Harth, Student, Pontifical College Josephinum, Columbus, OH
Donald R. Heiges, President Emeritus, Gettysburg Theological Seminary, Gettysburg, PA
Stanley Harakas, Former Dean, Holy Cross Greek Orthodox School of Theology, Brookline, MA
Henry Hildebrandt, Student, Pontifical College Josephinum, Columbus, OH
Douglas W. Hix, Director of Advanced Studies, Columbia Theological School, Decatur, GA
Carl Holladay, Faculty, Candler School of Theology, Emory University, Atlanta, GA
Philip Hower, Student, Pontifical College Josephinum, Columbus, OH
Donald L. Huber, Librarian, Trinity Lutheran Seminary, Columbus, OH
Alfred C. Hughes, Rector, St. John's Seminary, Brighton, MA
Rodney J. Hunter, Associate Professor of Pastoral Theology, Candler School of Theology, Emory University, Atlanta, GA
John Hurd, Director of Advanced Degrees, Trinity College, Toronto, Ontario, Canada
Oscar J. Hussel, Dean, Columbia Theological School, Decatur, GA
William Irwin, Dean, Faculty of Theology, University of St. Michael's College, Toronto, Ontario, Canada
Mary M. Janata, Program Director, Commission on Interprofessional Education, Ohio State University, Columbus, OH
C. Douglas Jay, Principal, Emmanuel College, Toronto, Ontario, Canada
Robert Kimbal, Dean, Star King School for Ministry, Berkeley, CA
Christa R. Klein, Former Professor, Gettysburg Theological Seminary, Gettysburg, PA
Pascal Klein, Student, Pontifical College Josephinum, Columbus, OH
Ralph Klein, Faculty, Lutheran Scool of Theology in Chicago, Chicago, IL
Victor Klimoski, Dean of Studies, St. Paul Seminary, St. Paul, MN
Benton Kline, Faculty, Columbia Theological Seminary, Decatur, GA
Matthew Kohmescher, S.M., Faculty, Department of Religious Studies, University of Dayton, Dayton, OH
Robert Kraft, Religion Department, University of Pennsylvania, Philadelphia, PA
Gerhard Krodel, Dean, Gettyburg Theological Seminary, Gettysburg, PA
Hilmer Krause, Professor, Episcopal Theological School of the Southwest, Austin, TX
James Kunde, The Kettering Foundation, Dayton, OH
Julian Kunie, Coordinator, Inter-racial and Cross Cultural Center, Graduate Theological Union, Berkeley, CA
Robert Lampert, Dean, Oblate School of Theology, San Antonio, TX
Jean-Marie Laporte, S.J., Dean, Regis College, Toronto, Ontario, Canada
William E. Lesher, President, Lutheran School of Theology at Chicago, Chicago, IL
Joseph Lind, Registrar and Business Manager, St. John's Seminary, Brighton, MA
John Linnan, C.S.V., President, Catholic Theological Union, Chicago, IL
Carl Linquist, President Emeritus, Christian College Consortium, St. Paul, MN
Robert W. Lynn, The Lilly Endowment, Indianapolis, IN
William Lynn, Acting Dean and Faculty, Pontifical College Josephinum, Columbus, OH
Durstan MacDonald, Dean, Episcopal Theological Scool of the Southwest, Austin, TX
Daniel F. Martensen, Director, Washington Theological Consortium, Washington, D.C.

Tony Martyn, Student, Pontifical College Josephinum, Columbus, OH
Donald Matthews, Librarian, Gettysburg Theological Seminary, Gettysburg, PA
Neeley McCarter, President, Pacific School of Religion, Berkeley, CA
Gordon B. McKeeman, President, Starr King School for the Ministry, Berkeley, CA
Francis Meehan, Former Faculty, Saint Charles Seminary, Philadelphia, PA
Arthur Merrill, Director of Library Services, United Theological Seminary, New
    Brighton, MN
A Berkeley Mickelsen, Bethel Theological Seminary, St. Paul, MN
Attila Mikloshazy, Dean of Studies, St. Augustine's Seminary, Scarborough, Ontario,
    Canada
Howard Mills, President, United Theological Seminary, New Brighton, MN
Jacques Monet, S.J., Regis College, Toronto, Ontario, Canada
Romney Mosley, Faculty, Candler School of Theology, Emory University, Atlanta,
    GA
Mary Pat Mulligan, Assistant to the Dean and Faculty, Pontifical College Josephinum,
    Columbus, OH
C. Ellis Nelson, President, Austin Presbyterian Theological Seminary, Austin, TX
Iain Nichol, Director, Toronto School of Theology, Toronto, Ontario, Canada
Joseph O'Neill, Conference of Small Private Colleges, Princeton, NJ
Kenneth O'Malley, Director of the Library, Catholic Theological Union, Chicago, IL
William T. Orlvey, S.J., Student, Toronto Scool of Theology, Toronto, Ontario
Kenan B. Osborne, O.F.M., President, Franciscan School of Theology, Berkeley, CA
Raymond O'Toole, Director, Institute for Social Ministry, Toronto School of
    Theology, Toronto, Ontario, Canada
John Padberg, President, Weston School of Theology, Cambridge, MA
John Patton, Executive Director, Georgia Association for Pastoral Care, Atlanta, GA
John Phelan, Dean of Students, North Park Theological Seminary, Chicago, IL
J. Davison Philips, President, Columbia Theological School, Decatur, GA
Joseph Plevnik, S.J., Regis College, Toronto, Ontario, Canada
William S. Pregnall, Dean and President, Church Divinity School for the Pacific,
    Berkeley, CA
Thomas J. Pugh, Vice President for Academic Services, Interdenominational
    Theological Center, Atlanta, GA
Calvin H. Reber, Jr., Director, Doctor of Ministry Program, United Theological
    Seminary, Dayton, OH
Gene Reeves, Dean, Medville/Lombard, Chicago, IL
John H. P. Reumann, Professor, The Lutheran Theological Seminary at Philadelphia,
    Philadelphia, PA
Rosemary Radford Ruether, Faculty, Garrett-Evangelical Theological Seminary,
    Evanston, IL
Lynn N. Rhodes, Director of Field Education, Pacific School of Religion, Berkeley,
    CA
Dawn Richards, Office Manager, Center for Women and Religion, Graduate
    Theological Union, Berkeley, CA
Nancy Richardson, Co-director, Women's Theological Center, Boston, MA
Marion Riley, C.S.J., Registrar, St. Paul Seminary, St. Paul, MN
Sharon Ringe, Faculty, Methesco, Delaware, OH

Michael Rion, President, Hartford Seminary, Hartford, CT
Pat Rocca, Former Student, Graduate Theological Union, Berkeley, CA
Nancy Roemheld, Student, Meadville/Lombard, Chicago, IL
Arthur E. Rodgers, Academic Dean, Religious Studies Division, St. Charles Seminary, Philadelphia, PA
Robert Roth, Faculty, Luther Northwestern Theological Seminary, St. Paul, MN
Randall T. Ruble, Vice President and Dean, Erskine Theological Seminary, Due West, SC
Anthony Saldarini, Faculty, Boston College, Chestnut Hill, MA
David Scholer, Dean, Northern Baptist Theological Seminary, Lombard, IL
David S. Schuller, Associate Director, Association of Theological Schools, Vandalia, OH
Edna Schultz, Registrar, Bethel Theological Seminary, St. Paul, MN
Dennis Sheehan, Rector, Pope John XXIII National Seminary, Weston, MA
Robert Shelton, Dean, Austin Presbyterian Theological Seminary, Austin, TX
Lloyd E. Sheneman, Director, Division of Professional Leadership, Lutheran Church in America, Philadelphia, PA
Anthony Shonis, Director of Spiritual Formation, Pontifical College Josephinum, Columbus, OH
Peter Slater, Faculty, Wycliffe College, Toronto, Ontario, Canada
Gerard S. Sloyan, Faculty, Temple University, Philadelphia, PA
Diane Snyder, Student, Toronto School of Theology, Toronto, Ontario, Canada
Graydon Snyder, Dean, Bethany Theological Seminary, Oak Brook, IL
Peter Somerville, Rector, St. Augustine's Seminary, Scarsborough, Ontario, Canada
John M. Stapleton, Director of D.Min. Program, Candler School of Theology, Emory University, Atlanta, GA
Clyde Steckel, Academic Vice-President, United Theological Seminary, New Brighton, MN
Harlan Stelmach, Director, Center for Ethics and Social Policy, Graduate Theological Union, Berkeley, CA
Alice Stroebel, Registrar, United Theological Seminary, New Brighton, MN
Florence Strobert, Secretary, Atlanta Theological Association, Candler School of Theology, Emory University, Atlanta, GA
Walter Stuhr, President, Pacific Lutheran Theological School, Berkeley, CA
Edward Sunderland, Student, Seabury-Western, Evanston, IL
Leonard Swidler, Faculty, Temple University, Philadelphia. PA
James Talentino, Student, Wycliffe College, Toronto, Ontario, Canada
David Tiede, Faculty, Luther Northwestern Theological Semiary, St. Paul, MN
John Tietjen, Faculty, Luther Northwestern Theological Seminary, St. Paul, MN
George B. Thomas, Faculty, Interdenominational Theological Center, Atlanta, GA
Gene M. Tucker, Faculty, Candler School of Theology, Emory University, Atlanta, GA
Arthur Unger, Planning Office, Graduate Theological Union, Berkeley, CA
Leo Van Everbroeck, C.I.C.M., Director, Graduate Division of Religion, LaSalle University, Philadelphia, PA
Anne Van Fossen, Board, Toronto School of Theology, Toronto, Ontario, Canada
Donald Vorp, Director of Library, McCormick Theological Seminary, Chicago, IL

James Waits, Dean, Candler School of Theology, Emory University, Atlanta, GA
Antoninus Wall, O.P., President, Dominican School of Philosophy and Theology, Berkeley, CA
Geraldine Warthling, O.S.F., Director of Field Education, Pontifical College Josephinum, Columbus, OH
Claude Welch, Dean, Graduate Theological Union, Berkeley, CA
Norman Wente, Director of the library, Luther Northwestern Theological Seminary, St. Paul, MN
Newell J. Wert, Vice President for Academic Affairs, United Theological Seminary, Dayton, OH
Donald Wiebe, Trinity College, Toronto, Ontario, Canada
Barbara Wheeler, President, Auburn Theological Seminary, New York, NY
Rufus Whitley, Director of Formation, Oblate Fathers, Oblate School of Theology, San Antonio, TX
Shelly Wiley, Student, Austin Presbyterian Theological Seminary, Austin, TX
Arthur Wood, Registrar, Toronto School of Theology, Toronto, Ontario, Canada
Jesse H. Ziegler, Faculty, United Theological Seminary, Dayton, OH

Paul Zywan, Student, Pontifical College Josephinum, Columbus, OH

JAMES W. FRASER is a member of the faculty of the College of Public and
Community Service and Senior Associate at the John W. McCormack
Institute of Public Affairs at the University of Massachusetts at Boston.
Among other studies, he is the author of *Pedagogue for God's
Kingdom: Lyman Beecher and the Second Great Awakening*
(University Press of America, 1985) and *Schooling the Preachers: The
Development of Protestant Theological Education in the United States,
1740-1875* (University Press of America, 1988). In addition, Dr. Fraser
is pastor of Grace Church, Federated, in East Boston, Massachusetts.

MONICA ELLEN FRIAR is currently a Municipal Planner in economic and
community development for IEP, Inc., an environmental planning firm
based in Sandwich, Massachusetts. Ms. Friar has strong data and
computer analysis skills which she developed initially at the Federal
Reserve Board while doing macroeconomic research.

BARBARA ANNE RADTKE is a member of the faculty of Emmanuel College in
Boston, Massachusetts, teaching in the Department of Theological
Studies and in the Department of Educational and Pastoral Ministry.
She is also on the permanent summer faculty of the Graduate Division
of Religious Education at LaSalle University. She lectures and gives
workshops to persons preparing for ministry. She is the author of
several articles about ministerial issues.

THOMAS J. SAVAGE, S.J. has recently been named President of Rockhurst
College, Kansas City, Missouri. He is the director and a trustee of
Cheswick Center in Belmont, Massachusetts. He is the author of *The
Governance of Catholic Health Care Institutions* (Catholic Health
Association, 1988), *The Cheswick Process: Seven Steps to a More
Effective Board* (The Lilly Endowment Inc. and Cheswick Center,
1981), *Neighborhood Revitalization and Religious Institutions*
(Cheswick Center and N Y City Planning Commission, 1979) and of
numerous articles.

KATARINA SCHUTH, O.S.F. is currently Director of Planning and Registrar at Weston School of Theology in Cambridge, Massachusetts. She is also the co-ordinator of a study on "The Futures of Catholic Theologates" funded by the Lilly Endowment, and author of a book *Reason for the Hope* (Michael Glazier, Inc., 1988), a book on the same topic, and of numerous articles. She serves as a trustee of several seminaries and other non-profit organizations.

INDEX

DATE DUE